Living the

Good Life

Living the Good Life

of a Christian Patriot

Roger Bynum

Roger Bynum

109 Gum Drive

Sherwood, AR 72120

Ordering Information:

Order   from   Amazon   or   contact   at: lacmusa@yahoo.com..

Living   the   Good   Life   of   a   Christian Patriot//Roger Bynum. —1st edition 2024

ISBN 979-8-218-55180-3

Dedicated to Aaron, Weston, Abigail, and Kellan

My son, forget not My law; but let your heart keep My commandments; for they shall add length of days, and long life, and peace, to you. Let not mercy and truth forsake you; tie them around your neck; write them upon the tablet of your heart; and you shall find favor and good understanding in the sight of God and man. Trust in the LORD with all your heart, and lean not to your own understanding. In all your ways acknowledge Him, and He shall direct your paths."—Proverbs 3:1-6

Acknowledgments

Many thanks to my dear Caraleen and to all the other godly men and women who by their examples and instruction helped me to learn the truths that are contained first in the Bible and now in this little book, and to Charlene who is walking with me now, sharing this final chapter of our lives. A special thanks to my friend, Darcy Pattison, for her help with editing, and publishing. I would never have gotten it done without her help. May God be glorified through His work in our lives.

"=all things, whatever you desire that men should do to you, do even so to them; for this is the Law and the Prophets.—Matthew 7:12

Contents

Introduction: A Letter to our Grandchildren

"I shall pass through this world but once. Any good therefore that I can do or any kindness that I can show to any fellow creature, let me do it now. Let me not defer or neglect it for I shall not pass this way again."----Stephen Grellet, 1772—1855

The entirety of this little essay is a letter I am writing to leave for my grandchildren and a few others whom I love and who call me "abuelo." I also have the vain hope that perhaps a few other people may find it useful.

Dear Aaron, Weston, Abigail, and Kellan:
This is from your Papaw, Chris and Steve's Dad, Roger Keith Bynum. I love you very much and I wish I could have had more time with you and had the opportunity just to enjoy being with you but also to talk with you about some of the things that I believe are important about life and how and why we make the choices and live as we do. The years I spent trying to share the gospel of Christ with the people of Mexico precluded that and even though I trust that was God's purpose and worthwhile, it was a great loss to me that I

1

had not more time with you. I trust your parents have talked with you about the following truths many timesbut repetition should do no harm. In the final section of the edition I prepared for you there is a bit more personal information about Caraleen, your grandmother, and myself.

Blessings,   Papaw (Roger Bynum)

Terminology

I will explain some of the terminology that I will use. You will note that I use the masculine gender when the case might be either. That has been correct English grammar for centuries. It is not correct to use "they, their, them [plural]" for a singular person, even though such errors are commonly made by semi-literate persons, some of whom are school-teachers, politicians, and media personalities! I will cite many passages from the Christian Bible and all such citations will be from the New King James version except where another source is indicated. Although not all agree, I believe that God the Holy Spirit breathed into and through the human authors of the Bible and they spoke or wrote nothing more. Therefore, in the original autographs the Bible is without error. I also believe that although there are errors in transmission in many versions of the scripture it was God's purpose to preserve His truth for us and because of that He superintended the translations so that by comparing scripture with scripture we can have confidence that the truth has been preserved for us.

The entire argument for the validity of Christianity rests upon the reliability of the scripture so I urge you to research the evidences for the divine origin of the Bible so you can have confidence in what you read there. Although an exhaustive study of the various evidences of the divine origin of the scripture are beyond the scope of this treatise it is immensely important that we have that confidence in the Bible so I will list in brief a few of those in the following pages and encourage you to research them for yourself for more detailed understanding.

Reasons to Believe the Bible

The Bible is the only comprehensive and authoritative source for Christianity and therefore for the principles I am giving you in this little book. Christians believe the events it reports actually occurred and that God speaks to us through its pages telling us Who He is, who we are, and how we are to live. There are various secular historians, authors, and archeologists who confirm significant details related to Israel that are reported in the Old Testament and concerning Jesus the Christ, Who is the sole focus of the New Testament in the gospels and the epistles. Only the Bible gives us a comprehensive understanding of Christianity and claims to be in its entirety, in the original autographs, the infallible Word of God. Why should we believe it to be true and give ourselves to Christ, following His teaching? I believe there are several good reasons that taken together make an overwhelming case for the validity of the Bible.

Historical Origin

The first reason to believe the Bible is its historical origin. The first five books of the Bible, called the Pentateuch, were written by Moses. We can't be precise, but there seem to have been about 2500 years from Adam, the first man, to Moses. There are no known written records of the events in that period, except the book of Job. Such records may have been lost, or they may have only been passed along through oral traditions.

According to Exodus, God came down and spoke to Moses on Mt. Sinai, giving him the Ten Commandments, and later gave him further revelations to direct the religious and civil life of Israel. After the time of Moses, God spoke to Israel through various judges and prophets. Numbers 1:46 says there were over 600,000 Israeli men who came out of Egypt with Moses, and that would indicate there were not less than 2,500,000 men, women, and children who had followed the presence of God manifested in a pillar of cloud by day and fire by night (Ex. 13:21, 22) and who were gathered around Mt. Sinai and witnessed the events that occurred there.

There is no evidence that there were any skeptics present who doubted the supernatural events that occurred that day, and for approximately the next 1600 years—until the birth of Christ—that revelation was accepted in Israel and generally guided the life of the nation.

Israel did not follow God's commandments perfectly and were disciplined by God, but I know of no writings from that period that challenged the authority and accuracy of Moses and the prophets. It has become more common in recent centuries for skeptics to deny the supernatural, assuming anything they have not witnessed and cannot explain could not possibly exist. However, if those witnesses accepted it then and for the next 1600 years, why should we today who are so far distant believe we have more reliable information and doubt those events?

Extraordinary Preservation

Through the years, powerful, diabolical opponents of God and Christianity have attempted to exterminate the Jewish people and to either destroy the Bible or make it inaccessible to ordinary people. They have been unable to do so because God had and has a purpose for Israel and for others who will trust in Christ. He preserves His Word to make that Good News known to humanity.

According to Wikipedia there are over 5800 complete or fragmented Greek manuscripts catalogued, 10,000 Latin manuscripts, and 9300 manuscripts in various other ancient languages. *None of the other ancient works of literature whose origins are commonly accepted compare with the New Testament in regard to the number of ancient manuscripts that have been preserved.*

Fulfilled Prophecy

Fulfilled prophecies are supernatural evidence of the divine origin of the Bible. These prophecies were given hundreds of years in advance of their fulfillment, many of them giving details about the Messiah—His birth, ministry, death, and resurrection—and others concerning other nations and rulers. The coming of the Messiah was clearly prophesied in the Old Testament (see Isaiah 7, 9, 53; Psalm 110; and many other passages) in very specific terms as many as 800 years before the birth of Jesus Christ in Bethlehem, but the first such prophecy was given in Genesis 3, right after the fall of mankind into sin. The four gospels, which are accounts of the life of Jesus Christ, and the epistles of the New Testament, confirm the fulfillment of hundreds of prophecies given in the Old Testament.

Internal Consistency

The internal consistency of the Bible is amazing and could hardly happen were God not guiding the human authors (2 Timothy 3:16, 17; 2 Peter 1:20, 21). The Bible consists of sixty-six books, thirty-nine in the Old Testament and twenty-seven in the New, written by some forty authors over a period of 1400 years treating thousands of years of historical events and complex life and theological issues—and all those books and authors are in complete agreement. There are people who deny that because they wish to discredit the Bible and will not or cannot read it with an unprejudiced view that is willing to acknowledge that apparent discrepancies have reasonable explanations, that there is an all-powerful and righteous Creator Who sustains the universe, does exactly what He chooses, and to whom we will all give account.

Moral Transparency

The transparency of the Bible, its honest disclosure of the flaws of some of its most honored patriarchs, is another strong argument in favor of its legitimacy. Can you imagine a contemporary organization voluntarily confessing that its leaders have engaged in lying, deceit, adultery, and murder expecting to attract adherents? That is what the Bible has done. Abraham, Isaac, Jacob, King David, and the apostle Peter (among others) are all shown to have done despicable things, not because those behaviors are approved but because God is Truth. The Bible shows its heroes with their "warts and all" because it is true and it is a book about grace and redemption.

Transforming Effect of the Gospel

I will cite only one other reason we should believe the Bible: the uplifting and transforming experiential effect that God's Word has had on people where it has been published. All through the centuries it has changed people from a selfish, evil character and made them moral and compassionate examples and defenders of truth and righteousness. Where the gospel has been preached the lot of women and children has been improved, hospitals are built, orphanages established, slavery abolished, and addicts have been set free.

I was controlled by vices I could not conquer until sixty years ago when I listened to gospel preaching and was drawn by God's Spirit to cast myself upon the merciful Savior who came "to seek and to save that which was lost." Christ received me and set me free, and I have served Him since that day, though certainly not as well as I should have. The psalmist said, "Oh, taste and see that the LORD is good . . . fear the LORD, you His saints! There is no want to those who fear Him (Psalm 34:8, 9)."

One should not expect to have one's curiosity satisfied concerning every question that can be raised. God gave us an adequate basis for our faith, but He did not give infinite knowledge to finite beings. The Bible tells us in four places, "The just shall live by faith," and God had and has no intention of eliminating the necessity of our trusting the good and gracious Creator who has shown Himself to be completely worthy of our trust.

What is the Good Life?

I hope with this essay to disabuse my readers of a misconception that was held a few years ago when it was common to hear one speak (or to read) about living the good life. That idea was understood to mean having become sufficiently affluent to have a large, luxurious residence (or several), expensive cars and boats, designer clothing, beautiful jewelry, and the ability to travel extensively, live a life of leisure, and indulge all one's desires. In short, the good life was conceived of as a self-centered life with no significant purpose other than to enjoy gratifying one's impulses.

I will concede there could be considerable pleasure in such a life for a while, but there is abundant evidence that the novelty soon wears away and new sources of entertainment must be found until the senses are dulled, health is destroyed, and one comes to the end of a life without purpose or hope. I would not call that "living the good life." I recommend you read the short little book of Ecclesiastes in the Old Testament of the Bible, apparently written by King Solomon, where he describes his experiences in seeking pleasure, happiness, wisdom, and meaning in life. Reading that book led me to repentance and trust in Jesus Christ.

I want further to recommend some life principles

found in the Christian Bible that we need to make an integral part of our character and that will then guide us in living a really worthwhile life. When these values (or principles—I will use these terms interchangeably) are widely followed, they tend to produce a peaceable, orderly, and just society, give honor to God, and bring His blessings upon us. This conviction that I hold will tell you something about who I am, but these principles are far more important than I am, or any man is, except the Lord Jesus Christ.

At this juncture, in the unhappy event that anyone who might read this essay should become weary and not finish it, I want right here to urge you to a course of action which, if you take it, will be the most important thing you will do in your life and will have an enormous impact on who you are and everything else you will do.

The Good News of Life in Jesus Christ

I want to tell you about the good news of what God has done for us in Christ, but that message can mean nothing to us unless we understand the horrible and hopeless predicament of mankind without God. So first I must tell you some very bad news.

Due to something that happened thousands of years before we were born, over which we had no control, we were born into a race, the human race, that was and is alienated from God (Genesis 1–3). Our instinct has been to seek our own path, to want to be independent of everyone, and submit to no authority, and that includes the omnipotent, good, and gracious God who created us, gives us life and breath, and sustains us each moment (Colossians 1:12, 17).

Isaiah said, "All we like sheep have gone astray, we have turned everyone to his own way (Isaiah 53:6)." The apostle Paul said, "All have sinned and come short of the glory of God (Romans 3:23 KJV)." That means we have deliberately done what we knew we ought not do, we've failed to do what we knew we should, and, because of our nature, we have been unable to perceive the glory, majesty, and perfection that belongs to God.

We have not understood how indescribably fortunate it would be to know Him and have Him direct our lives. We were spiritually "dead in trespasses and sins (Ephesians 2:1)," enemies of God, unwilling and unable to love and submit to the will of God (Romans 8:7). "There is none righteous, no, not one; There is none who understands; There is none who seeks after God (Romans 3:10, 11)."

That was our condition in our fallen, depraved state, the way we were born. We were powerless to change unless someone could and would intervene to help us. Were nothing done to remedy our desperate plight, we all would continue forever in the torment of separation from the One who is the source of all life and joy. But "God, [who is] full of compassion, gracious, longsuffering, and plenteous in mercy and truth," intervened for us to do what no one else could (Psalm 86:15 KJV; Ephesians 2:1, 5). (1) He sent His Son, Jesus Christ, to save us, (2) He told us how we can benefit from the work that Christ did, and (3) He told us how we can know that we have peace with God.

Jesus Christ, the eternal and unique Son of God, was born of the virgin Mary, grew up to be a man, and lived a sinless life fulfilling all the righteousness of the law of God. He then took our sin upon Himself and died

14

in our place on the cross so that those who trust in Him will be forgiven and never be punished for their sin (John 10:17, 18; Romans 5:8, 9). Equally important, He gives us new life and a new mentality so that we can perceive the glory of God and understand the blessedness of trusting and following Him (John 6:35; Matthew 11:28–30: Psalm 119:165). "For He made Him who knew no sin to be sin for us, that we might become the righteousness of God in Him (2 Corinthians 5:21)."

After his death Christ was buried, but on the third day He rose again demonstrating His deity and showing that His sacrifice for us was accepted by God the Father and we are forever justified (Romans 4:25: 1 Corinthians 15:1–4). After forty days, Jesus visibly ascended into heaven and is seated at the right hand of the Father where He constantly and forever intercedes with the Father for those who by grace through faith have been made part of the family of God (Acts 1:9; Luke 24:51; Romans 8:34; Hebrews 7:25). The Scriptures tell us how we come to have the benefit of Christ's work and become children of God.

Christ said, "No one can come to Me unless the Father who sent Me draws him; and I will raise him up at the last day (John 6:44)." He also said, "All that the Father gives Me will come to Me, and the one who comes to Me I will by no means cast out (John 6:37)." Christ tells us that we must repent, have a change in our thoughts, values, and attitudes. He said, "I tell you, no; but unless you repent you will all likewise perish (Luke 13:5)." Acts 3:19 says, "Repent therefore and be converted, that your sins may be blotted out." Acts 11:18 tells us that it is God who grants repentance. When we are without spiritual life, unable to appreciate goodness and truth, enemies of God, He gives us a new spiritual birth (Ephesians 2:1, 5; 1 Peter 1:3–23). By means of the Holy Spirit, Christ the Creator comes to us and makes an internal change in us: in our intellect, our affections, and our will. We begin turning away from our own proud and selfish way and start following Christ. "As many as received Him, to them He gave the right to become children of God, to those who believe in His name: who were born, not of blood, nor of the will of the flesh, nor of the will of man, but of God (John 1:12, 13)."

Christ said He "came to seek and to save that which was lost" (Luke 19:10), and He illustrated that in Luke 15, explaining how the shepherd goes out to find the lost sheep and bring it into the fold. The apostle Paul sums up much of this in Ephesians 2:8–10 where he says, "For by grace you have been saved through faith, and that not of yourselves; it is the gift of God not of works, lest anyone should boast. For we are His workmanship, created in Christ Jesus for good works, which God prepared beforehand that we should walk in them." That is an accurate theological explanation of conversion from the perspective of the sovereign, gracious work of God in the new birth. One who is saved, given new spiritual life, forgiven all sins, and who begins to follow Christ, does so only because of the unmerited favor of God and the miraculous transforming power of God's Spirit working within him, not because of any goodness in himself that earned God's kindness. "Therefore, if anyone is in Christ, he is a new creation; old things have passed away; behold, all things have become new (II Cor. 5:17)."

The practical explanation of the change in attitude and behavior which God produces in the one who is given new life is shown in Romans 10:9–17: "[If] you confess with your mouth the Lord Jesus and believe in your heart that God has raised Him from the dead, you will be saved. For with the heart one believes unto righteousness, and with the mouth confession is made unto salvation." For the Scripture says, 'Whoever believes on Him will not be put to shame.' For there is no distinction between Jew and Greek, for the same Lord over all is rich to all who call upon Him. For 'whoever calls on the name of the LORD shall be saved.'

How then shall they call on Him in whom they have not believed? And how shall they believe in Him of whom they have not heard? And how shall they hear without a preacher? And how shall they preach unless they are sent? As it is written: 'How beautiful are the feet of those who preach the gospel of peace, who bring glad tidings of good things!' But they have not all obeyed the gospel. For Isaiah says, 'Lord, who has believed our report?' So then faith comes by hearing, and hearing by the Word of God."

That may be a bit complex and difficult to follow, so I will now give a very brief summary. We were all without spiritual life, separated from God by our sin, with no desire or ability to come to God. But for His own purposes and glory He chose to redeem a remnant of humanity and sent His Son Jesus to die for their sins and reconcile them to God. He ordained that the good news of Christ's work and its benefit for His people would be preserved in the Bible and spread through those whom He had chosen, telling others about Christ and His gift of salvation to those who will trust in Him. He then sends the Holy Spirit to each person whom He has chosen and grants him or her a new spiritual birth so that when His chosen ones hear the gospel they are convinced of their sin and the justice of God in punishing their sin. But at the same time, they believe that Christ died for their sin and that each one who comes, embracing Him is forgiven, has peace with God, and the gift of unending life with God.

But now a critical matter: how can one know that he has that genuine trust in Christ that receives God's grace, forgiveness, and everlasting life? Even after we are converted and begin to follow Christ, we sometime stumble and sin, and then we may ask ourselves, can I really be a child of God? How can I know? The apostle John gives a clear answer to that question in his first letter by giving three proofs (some find four) that one really does know Christ in an intimate way and has been born anew spiritually.

(1) John says in 1 John 2:3, "Now by this we know that we know Him, if we keep His commandments." I know of no one who believes that this means the regenerate perfectly keep all the commands and the will of God in every detail and all the time—we are not yet perfectly holy and beyond sinning. Rather, it means that the redeemed love God—Father, Son, and Holy Spirit—that they love His Word and believe it to be the best rule for our lives, and that the predominant characteristic of their lives is obedience to God, not disobedience (1 John 5:2).

(2) He then says in 1 John 3:14, "We know that

we have passed from death to life, because we love the brethren. He who does not love his brother abides in death." Unregenerate men are naturally selfish and usually manipulate and exploit others to gain what they wish. Genuine love that puts the welfare of another ahead of oneself is really rare among those who do not know Christ. But Jesus commanded us to love God with all our being, to love our neighbor as we love ourselves, and even to love our enemies, and through the Holy Spirit He puts His own love within us to enable us to do that. Jesus said, "By this all will know that you are My disciples, if you have love for one another." (John 13:35)

(3) These first two proofs are objective and observable, but then John gives us a subjective proof. In 1 John 4:13 he says, "By this we know that we abide in Him, and He in us, because He has given us of His Spirit." Romans 8:15, 16 amplifies that when the apostle Paul speaks of "the Spirit of adoption by whom we cry out, 'Abba, Father.'" He then says, "The Spirit Himself bears witness with our spirit that we are children of God." The Holy Spirit living in us gives us a sense that we have peace with God, that we belong to Him; that I am His child and He is my Father (see Hebrews 13:6). "Let us therefore come boldly to the throne of grace, that we may obtain mercy and find grace to help in time of need." (Hebrews 4:16)

Dearly beloved, I pray that you will come to Christ, confessing your sins, asking for forgiveness, and believing that Christ died to save you. If you genuinely do that, it will not just mean that you don't have to worry about punishment for your sin or that you will attend worship services more or less frequently. It will be the beginning of a new life of loving, trusting, and serving Christ, living to honor Him, and serving others in His name. "If anyone is in Christ he is a new creation; old things are passed away; behold, all things are become new (II Corinthians 5:17)."

In the following pages I will talk with you about a number of values or principles that are part of the character of Christ and that He wants to form in our own character (Philippians 2:5; Romans 8:29). I hope my discussion will help you toward that goal, but there is one course of action which will, if you take it, be more useful than everything else I will say in the following pages.

The Basics: Read the Bible and Seek God in Prayer Daily

Read all of the Bible systematically, again and again, study it, let few days pass when you do not, when you feel devout and when you don't, because it is the one means we can trust through which God speaks to us. It tells us who God is, who we are, what God wants of us, how we can be forgiven, how to have peace with God and eternal life. It changes us and gives us profound wisdom for living and managing the challenges of life. Read the Bible alone, and when you have a spouse and children, do it with them daily and teach them to do it. Pray when you read the Bible, and read the Bible when you pray. All the people you know or will know who have made shipwreck of their lives have done so because they were not taught and/or did not prayerfully study and follow the teachings of the Bible. I could tell you of several such persons whom I know personally. None of us do as well as we could if we were more careful and disciplined in following God's Word.

Where I live near Little Rock, Arkansas, I know of four churches of 300 to 500 in attendance whose numbers shrank until they closed their doors (others are nearing the same end). I am convinced this happens because it is almost certain that fewer than 30% of professing Christians are serious enough about listening to and obeying the voice of God to regularly read and study their Bibles. When we regularly meditate on the Word of God, we will become strong in faith with the consequence that we will live, not perfect lives, but lives that are uniquely different from most of the society around us in that we will model truth, love, humility, and biblical righteousness, and will be zealous to share the gospel regularly with those around us. This will produce life and growth in the church.

The following four verses are among many which show us what God's Word does in our lives.

"Your word is a lamp to my feet, and a light to my path (Psalm 119:105)."

"Your word I have hidden in my heart, that I might not sin against you (Psalm 119:11)."

"For the word of God is living and powerful, and sharper than any two-edged sword, piercing even to the division of soul and spirit, and of joints and marrow, and is a discerner of the thoughts and intents of the heart (Hebrews 4:12)."

"Great peace have those who love Your law, and nothing causes them to stumble (Psalm 119:165)."

Don't Procrastinate: Your Life is Passing Rapidly

Having commended to you the practice of daily reading the Scripture and praying, let me urge you to begin that practice at once. Be prompt, and be zealous, and delight in quickly obeying God, not wasting years and opportunities while seeking the pleasures of the world. Many people resolve to do good things but at another time that might seem more convenient because they are presently occupied with things that seem urgent or that they enjoy more. Reading and learning the Word of God, and prayer, are spiritual disciplines and thus they require discipline. They are hard on the selfish and corrupt ego, but they develop strength in the spirit. The potential gain from Bible study and prayer that is lost when they are neglected can never be recovered, but much sorrow and regret can be caused by their neglect.

Now let's continue with the specific life principles to which I alluded above. In some cases, I will cite passages of Scripture that command us to live a certain way and elaborate on it. In other cases, when I believe the application is obvious, I will leave you to observe it. I believe these values or principles are actually attributes or qualities of God that we should seek to embody because we want to be like Him. The one exception is the quality of humility. God is not humble except as the Son, in His humanity. It would be totally inappropriate for the Father to be humble: He is majestic and awesome!

The Struggle with the World, the Flesh, and the Devil

You should not believe I am pretending to be the best example of these values—just that I believe them with all my heart and aspire to follow them. Every day I confess my sins to our Lord and ask Him to pardon me and enable me to do better than the previous day. I believe obedience to Christ is the best way I or anyone else can give real evidence of faith in God, honor and please Him, and also serve his family, neighbor, country, and world. I believe the embodiment and practice of these values we will discuss are clearly taught in the Holy Bible, God's Word, but I do not believe it is adequate for us just to assume because we read the Word of God with our children that we, and they, will automatically acquire these values. *The residue of sinful nature within us keeps dragging us in the other direction, and we must fight against it!*

We fight against the residue of sin that is in us (what the apostle Paul called "putting to death our old nature") by, first, being very intentional about identifying our weaknesses and the qualities that God wants us to develop and that we want our children, others whom we love, and really everybody to have. And then, secondly, we must develop and employ a variety of tactics to inculcate these values. I believe it is not an overstatement to say if everyone constantly displayed these characteristics, strife would be eliminated from the world (James 4:1–3**).**

Of course, we know that will not happen until Christ returns and our sanctification (absolute and complete separation from sin/evil) is complete, but our practice of spiritual disciplines, and our striving for that end while knowing we are completely dependent on His grace to get there, is a necessary part of that process of becoming more like our Lord Jesus. So, we read the Word of God, we learn "what God is like" and how He wants us to be, and then we use all our ingenuity and all the teaching and learning tools we possess, including the support of our brethren in the church, day after day and year after year, to shape ourselves and others, constantly pleading that He will make our efforts effective, and form us in the image of His Son Jesus Christ (Romans 8:29).

God; the Bible, God's Word; Truth; the Foundation of All

The apostle Paul says in Colossians concerning Christ that *"by Him were all things created [made from nothing] . . . and He is before all things and by Him all things consist [cohere, are held together, sustained]* (Colossians 1:16, 17)." All that is true whether we are speaking of God the Father, Jesus the Son of God, or of the Spirit of God. When Moses asked God what he should tell Israel when they wanted to know who is this god that sent you, God said of himself, "I AM WHO I AM." I think that meant, "I am the only one who is self-existent, uncreated; and I Am the Creator and source of all else that is." Paul Tillich, called this "the ground of being." Everything that exists was created and is sustained by God.

There is *The Truth*, Christ, and there are discrete glimpses of truth, reality, that God enables us to grasp. The first truth I want to talk about is that *there is Truth*, and we should be committed to it. Jesus said, "I am the Way, the Truth, and the Life (John 14:6**)."** We should be committed to learning the truth, maintaining it, speaking it, and doing what we have said we will do. That does not mean we should always tell everything we know. Sometimes another person does not have the need to know what you or I know, and for us to tell them could be harmful, but we should never engage in deceit and tell something that we know is false. That is a lie, and the Bible condemns it in the strongest terms. It says liars (those who habitually lie and do not repent and embrace the truth) will have their part in the lake of fire. Most of us at some time will find it very inconvenient to speak the truth. Whether we do or do not speak the truth indicates whether we are really trusting Christ at that moment. Such times are a test of our spiritual life.

There are humanists, many teaching in our universities, who argue that there is no absolute truth nor absolute standard of right and wrong; that everything is relative and a matter of preference. That is a lie of Satan designed to destroy gullible people. Few of its purveyors are able to maintain it when they are themselves suffering or a victim of wrongdoing.

Why is the truth so important? I believe it is because the truth is an accurate description of reality, and without being able to accurately perceive reality we could not know what we should do and what results our behavior would produce—the world would be, or appear to be, completely chaotic and unpredictable. We could not trust anybody or anything, we would not know God, and the world would be a very terrifying place.

God is not like that. His Word, the Bible, is true in its entirety—even though we find things there that are difficult to understand, which in turn provide us an occasion to trust Him (Romans 1:17). There are many things about science and technology of which the Bible says nothing, but it is the absolute standard of truth on every matter about which it speaks, and most importantly, about spiritual matters, our relationship to God, other people, and eternity. God makes Himself known to us, He is unchangeable, and we can trust Him. "Jesus said, I am the Way, the Truth, and the Life; no one comes to the Father but by me (John 14:6)." "Jesus Christ is the same yesterday, today, and forever (Hebrews 13:8)." We should be becoming like Him (Romans 8:29; 2 Corinthians 3:17), and therefore we should speak the truth and perform our words.

Right and Wrong

In the Bible, God tells us what is right and what is wrong. There will be many times in your life when you will have to choose whether you will do right or wrong. You know people who seem more inclined to do what is right and others what is convenient. I hope you have already chosen to do right—always. If you have, it will make it a little easier to make that same choice when you are confronted with individual situations where the pressure is on and you are tempted to do wrong. We all have those tests and temptations. It is not wrong to be tempted; it is wrong to give in to evil. We will all fail sometimes and need to repent, which means to recognize and acknowledge I did wrong, desire to change, and to ask God to forgive me and enable me to avoid doing so again. It is vitally important that we resolve always to choose to live for and honor God, and ask Him to give us grace (His undeserved favor) to enable us to choose and do what is right.

The Bible tells us that when the first man, Adam, was created, God gave him only one commandment, and it was that he not eat the fruit from a given tree—a tree that, should he eat of it, would not only give him the "knowledge of good and evil" but also bring about his death. The giving of that commandment teaches us there

31

is One who is our source and has the wisdom and authority to command, that we are to trust and obey Him absolutely, and that we have no reason to doubt our trusting and obeying Him will produce the best of all possibilities for us. The issue was not that God did not want Adam to have intelligence and wisdom; it was that He wanted Him first to have the highest and most essential wisdom of knowing and trusting His Creator completely. When one does that, God will then guide him into the other truths and wisdom that he needs to acquire.

You notice I did not begin by telling you there is a Creator God and attempting to prove that, even though that is the most basic truth beneath everything else. The reason I did not is because the Bible says every person has that knowledge in its most basic elemental form within himself, even though he (or she) may lack much understanding of the attributes and will of God and how to know Him and please Him. We do know there is right and wrong, and something—Someone—makes it so. *We know enough to give us reason to seek the answers to those questions: Who is God, what is He like, and how should I live? If one does not do so, it is because he would prefer not to have those answers and not to have to give account to that authority (although one can never succeed in that—we will all give account to God).*

One prefers to be the ultimate authority over his own life and do as he pleases. God calls that rebellion *sin*, when one wishes to be independent from Him who is each moment the source of our breath and life, the One who gave His Son to suffer and die to redeem sinners.

Left to our own resources we would never seek God or live righteous lives, *the good life!* The apostle Paul tells us in Romans 3 that, left to our own resources, "there is none righteous, no not one, there is none who understands, none who seeks after God." We only begin to seek God when the Lord Jesus Christ, the Good Shepherd, first comes seeking and finding the one He has chosen to be His sheep (Luke 19:10; John 6:44; John 10:26) and with His Word and His Spirit He makes a change within us so that we begin to love Him who loved us first. He chooses and saves us not because of anything within us but just because that is who He is and that is what He, who always does Good and what He chooses, chose to do.

Please read and study the first two chapters of Ephesians and memorize Ephesians 2:8–10. I will leave you a list of other passages that teach important truths and that I remember well. I hope you will decide it is worthwhile to read the Bible frequently and hide much of its truths in your mind and heart. You should search and learn for yourself the difference between the mind and the spiritual "heart" of man (Romans 10:9, 10).

We are born as sinners into a fallen world, and even after we have come to know and trust in Christ, the process of our spiritual growth in becoming like Christ will not immediately be finished but will continue all of our mortal lives. As it does, we will be tempted (like Adam was) to trust our own judgment and do things we know are wrong, and sometime we will succumb to the temptation; that is sin. God will forgive sin (not trusting and obeying Him) when He has brought us to repentance, that is, coming to despise the sin and earnestly desiring and resolving never to return to it, but nonetheless sin always has negative consequences. Sometimes the temporal consequences are enormous and obvious, and other times less so—but we can never tell in advance what they will be, and we should never treat wrongdoing as a trivial thing.

I urge you now to resolve to always trust Christ; believe He is God the Son, that He died and paid for the sins of those who trust in Him, and that His will and purpose for us is always the best of all possible options. Never deliberately do what you know is wrong or fail to do what you know you should do. *When one is intensely dissatisfied with things about his or her own behavior, thoughts, attitudes, and words,* whether they occur frequently or less often, and strives to change those things, asking the Lord's help to do so, knowing we can never by our own effort be pleasing to God and deserve anything good from Him, that is usually an indication that God is working within us, changing our nature, causing us to trust and love Him, and drawing us to Himself.

We have two challenges in doing what is right. One is knowing what is right: what I ought to do or refrain from doing. I said above that we have within us a basic understanding of right and wrong, and that is true. But sometimes we are confronted with two courses of action, and it seems they are equally good or equally bad, and we must choose to do one and not the other. When that occurs it is important that we already have the wisdom of God's Word within us and that we pray and look to Him to guide us in our decision and enable us to know what we ought to do.

The other problem in always choosing to do what is right, when we have determined what that is, is that for selfish reasons we may be tempted to do what is wrong. The right may require discipline and hard work—and we may be lazy, self-indulgent, and prefer to take the easy course. The wrong choice may appear to offer us experiences that we think we would enjoy immensely, and we want to indulge ourselves, that is, not to deny our impulses for pleasure. Choosing to do right may bring others to disapprove or persecute us. *If you are going to live the good life that is pleasing to God and useful to those around you, so that at the end of life you will know you have used your opportunity and lived well and not be filled with shame and regret, then you will need to commit yourself now to seek the wisdom to know what is right in each decision and for God's grace to follow a life of self-discipline, doing what is right and of eternal value, not just what feels good at the moment and seems convenient.* Neither you, me, or any exclusively mortal human being will do that perfectly, but we should aspire to do so, and it could and should be the preponderant example of our life. When we stumble and do less, but repent, God will forgive us, and we can begin anew (1 John 1:7–10; 2:1).

Religious Works Are Useless to Save: Only Christ Can Save Us

Living the truly good life, doing right, having God's approval and blessing, begins when He produces in us a recognition and heart-felt regret that because of our sin we deserve his judgment (Romans 3:23). He grants us a desire and resolve to choose and do right and in so doing to honor Him, and He gives us confidence in the good news of the gospel that Christ has borne the sins of all who will trust in Him (Romans 6:23). If you have not already done that, I pray you will do it now.

Others can teach you but no one can do this for you. You may do it at any time or place when God grants you a strong compulsion to seek Him, to turn from your own way and give your life to Christ, but know this is not a trivial thing, and if you come to Christ in this way you will be changed and in some very significant ways (like wanting to be pleasing to Christ) and you will never again be as you were before. If that change does not occur, then you just engaged in a useless religious ritual (II Cor. 5:17).

Now let me talk with you a little about some of the truths that you will find in those books that I've chosen and given you and that I believe are important in life. I think life in this world as God designed it has many harmonious parts—everything "fits" together, and many truths are linked to others. So when I talk about one truth or principle, it may seem I wander into matters that are hardly related, but I hope you will be able to see the reason and that my logic won't be too difficult to follow—and of course I will repeat myself, but when I do, the point usually merits emphasis.

The Biblical Charge to Discipleship and Making Disciples

In the following passages, our Lord charges us to follow Him and to invite, urge, train, and persuade others to do so. We will note several features that are common to each succeeding passage.

Deuteronomy 6:4–7: *"Hear, O Israel: The Lord our God, the Lord is one! You shall love the Lord your God with all your heart, with all your soul, and with all your strength. And these words which I command you today shall be in your heart. You shall teach them diligently to your children, and shall talk of them when you sit in your house, when you walk by the way, when you lie down, and when you rise up."*

Joshua 1:8: *"This Book of the Law shall not depart from your mouth, but you shall meditate in it day and night, that you may observe to do according to all that is written in it. For then you will make your way prosperous, and then you will have good success."*

Proverbs 22:6: *"Train up a child in the way he should go, and when he is old he will not depart from it."*

Psalm 86:15: *"But You, O Lord, are a God full of compassion, and gracious, longsuffering, and abundant* *in mercy and truth."*

The preeminent truth these verses show, and that we must inculcate, is that there is an omnipotent, good, and compassionate God who created us and the entire universe. He has shown his existence in His creation but revealed much more about Himself and His purposes for us in the Bible, His written Word. He commands us to love, trust, and obey Him and train our children to do so, and, ultimately, we will give account to Him for whether or not we do so. God gives us specific commands about some of the practices we are to utilize to learn of Him and train our children in His ways.

In the Joshua passage He says we are to meditate on His Word day and night, as well as speak of it and teach it to our children, and that doing so will bring prosperity and success. Remember, these are general principles; they are not promises that account for God's sovereign work in a given life (like Job's) at every moment. Most of the principles in Proverbs are in this category.

The Deuteronomy passage, as our Lord Jesus in His teaching, makes it clear that the most important truth we are to learn and teach is who God is and that we are to fear Him, love Him, and serve Him. We must embrace these truths with all our being. If we do not, then it will be useless for us to attempt to teach them to others. But after we are thoroughly convinced of these truths, then we are to seize every opportunity, in all our activities with our family (and others) to teach these eternally established principles. We are to explain how these truths about God and His Word guide our beliefs, our attitudes, and our behavior, beginning when we rise in the morning (a good time to read the Bible and pray together) and continuing until day's end.

Let me ask you, beloved, especially if you think of yourself as a believer in Jesus and one of His followers: *Are you doing this?* If not, you are disobeying God and wasting precious opportunities to invest in the well-being of your spouse and children. In all our activities of the day, when we are out in public with our children, making choices and interacting with other people, we are to recall to our children passages from the Word of God that we have previously read and remembered, explaining to them, "This is why we respect and help others as we do, and why we avoid doing things that many other people do that are contrary to the Word of God and that neither honor God nor our neighbor." Then, when we have returned to our homes, we continue to be guided by the Word of God in our family activities and as we conclude the day with Bible reading and prayer, confessing our sins and asking forgiveness, and giving thanks for all the good things, loved ones, neighbors, and friends we have received from God's hand. We can do none of these things unless we make deliberate life and career choices that will give us a lot of time with our family, and unless we then use that time wisely.

Training our children as Proverbs 22 commands involves teaching them the truths and principles of the Word of God just as the other passages indicate but also giving them an example of our own love for God, our own glad obedience to his Word, and our love for our own family and our neighbors (who, according to Christ, include everyone who needs a neighbor). Finally, training our children includes disciplining them as is needed to require obedience of them so they will develop the habit of making good choices.

Psalm 86:15 is to remind us that God is a good and gracious Father, and when we have failed in these things (as we sometimes will) and we repent, He will forgive us. Then it is time for a new and better beginning. That passage also reminds us that when things are not going the way that seems good to us, God is still in control and He is doing good even though we do not understand how current events could possibly produce good. Then is the time to remember that the

Bible says in four places, beginning in Habakkuk, "The just shall live by faith," and in Romans 10:17, "Faith comes by hearing the Word of God." It is also good to remember that when God has begun a good work in us, He will never despair and abandon it or us but will bring it to completion (Philippians 1:6), and there is nothing in all creation that can ever separate those whom He has chosen from God's love given to us in Christ Jesus (Romans 8:38, 39).

Some tools we will use for our own spiritual development (to enable us to live the truly good life) as well as to train our children and others whom we can teach/disciple include: 1) reading regularly and extensively in the Bible (as indicated above), and also, 2) presenting to our "students" the list of values we have previously identified in the Bible, reviewing them together, and asking them to help us find them in the Scripture during our regular reading.

What Is Important in Life: How Should One Live?

Since I propose to advise people on how they should live, it is only appropriate that I reference my authority for doing so. Why should you believe what I am saying? I hope to explain in brief something that is said on this matter in the Bible by the omniscient, omnipotent, and Holy Being who created the universe. You should believe Him! I pray He will enable me to cite his Word faithfully and to explicate it without error.

The Bible teaches that all mankind are sinners, we have fallen from God's favor, and we have neither the ability nor desire to seek and know God (Romans 3: 6–8) until He comes to us, finds us, and recreates us, changing us internally, bringing us back to Him Who is love, truth, and righteousness (John 15: 16; Genesis 3:1–9; Luke 15:3–7). We are not saved by or because of any intrinsic value in us or anything we can do but by grace, God's favor that we do not deserve, that He gives us in Christ, and we receive simply by trusting in Him (Ephesians 2:8, 9). Those whom He saves are not saved by their own works, but they are saved to do good works, and because God has ordained that those in whom his Spirit lives will inevitably do good (Ephesians 2:10), although not in each and every moment of our lives because we are still imperfect, still being changed by degrees to be like Christ (Romans 8:29). The similarity is sometimes less than it should be, the process of change painfully slow, but God never fails in His designs. What He began He absolutely will bring to perfection (Philippians 1:6), and the works we do will be similar to those Christ has done (John 14:12).

Several notable men of faith, patriarchs of Israel and icons of the church, have had shameful moments when they failed God and caused great injury and sorrow. Those awful examples given in Scripture add to its authenticity and warn us from similar failure, but they also give us hope in God's merciful kindness when we have stumbled and might despair were it not for them. But we should remember those failures were not typical of God's people; they were exceptions in what were otherwise admirable lives. John makes it clear that sin (defiance, selfishness, malice) is not usually characteristic of God's people (1 John 3:1–10). The Christian will sometimes stumble into sin, but he cannot long remain in it and be content. The greater the interval in which a person continues unrepentant in sin, the less reason there is for confidence, on the part of that person or others, that such person has experienced a new birth, no matter their past or present profession (1 John 2:3; 3:14).

We should remember that sin is not only transgression of a specific prohibition in God's Word but also the failure to comply with all the positive commands, duties, and responsibilities God has given us. "Therefore, to him who knows to do good and does not do it, to him it is sin (James 4:17)." James also said, "But someone will say, 'You have faith, and I have works.' Show me your faith without your works, and I will show you my faith by my works. You believe that there is one God. You do well. Even the demons believe—and tremble! But do you want to know, O foolish man, that faith without works is dead (James 2:18–20)?"

So as Christians, followers of Christ, where does that leave us? It leaves us with grateful hearts that Christ has taken our sins and given us His righteousness and that He will never leave us (2 Corinthians 5:21). It leaves us loving Him and those about us, wanting to obey Him and help those who need our help, and with confidence that He will enable us to do that. Finally, it gives us the responsibility to think soberly and plan carefully to determine what are those things we need to be doing, in our families, in our church, with our neighbors, in our work, and as citizens of our country, and to get about it because time is "a-wastin'" and we will give account for how we use it. "And let us consider one another to provoke unto love and to good works

(Hebrews 10:24, KJV)?" Let's think now about spiritual disciplines that God has given us to make us more like Christ and help us in living the truly good life.

Spiritual Disciplines

For decades the term *spiritual disciplines* has not been in common use in much of the Church, so you may not have heard it. The church, the people of God, have been poorer as a result. Spiritual disciplines are those exercises, or practices, that God has given us in His Word to strengthen us and enable us to make wise choices and overcome temptation. They help us to follow Christ. Toward the first of this dissertation I told you that the greatest battle you will have is that of resisting your less-than-admirable impulses and choosing to do what you know is right, even when it is difficult and requires much determination. God has given us spiritual disciplines to strengthen and aid us in that very difficult task. These disciplines are clearly commanded in the Bible, and I rather doubt one can really be a Christian and ignore these commands. I know such a person will have little success in living the Christian life, honoring God, and helping others to do so. I will enumerate those disciplines that are most essential. But first, let me say a bit about two important concepts.

Integrity and Virtue

One might almost say that a person of integrity

needs nothing more since the concept implies being strong, upright, and complete in character. One problem with the idea that integrity alone is enough is that the concept is not in common use today and not well understood. Also, since it is such a broad overarching quality, our memories are so poor, and we are easily distracted from the essential to the trivial, that like the Ten Commandments and the Beatitudes, the concept of integrity requires a lot of application to have an impact in our lives. It is also true that integrity does not necessarily include a monotheistic understanding of God, nor of Jesus as the God-man, who is the only One who redeems us from sin and through trust in Him reconciles us to God giving us eternal life.

Having virtue is having moral qualities and that term alone is not specific enough to guide us in determining what sort of people we are to be and how we are to live. In the discussion below about biblical values I will attempt to develop the specific virtues that a person of integrity should have and demonstrate in living the good life; a life that is useful to our neighbors and that gives tribute to the glory of the only omnipotent, good, compassionate, and righteous Creator.

Give Priority to the Word of God

The first spiritual discipline is frequently (usually daily) reading, studying, and meditating on God's Word, the Bible. There are many passages in the Bible that command us to do so.

Deuteronomy 6:5–7 says, "You shall love the LORD your God with all your heart, with all your soul, and with all your strength. And these words which I command you today shall be in your heart. You shall teach them diligently to your children, and shall talk of them when you sit in your house, when you walk by the way, when you lie down, and when you rise up."

In nineteen passages in the gospels Christ says, "Follow Me," and the only way we can do that is by reading, learning, and obeying His word. "My sheep hear My voice, and I know them, and they follow Me (John 10:27)." "If any one serves Me, let him follow Me (John 12:26)." "And He said to them all, 'If any man desires to come after Me, let him deny himself, and up his cross daily, and follow Me (Luke 9:23)." A person who is not serious about at least trying to obey Christ is not a Christian and has no biblical basis for believing he has peace with God (Luke 14:26–33).

Besides this minimal level of obedience to Christ, there are several other reasons why it is so important for us to internalize the precepts of the Word of God. It contains vital information about Who God is, what He is like, who we are, what His purposes are for us, what He has done to enable us to achieve His purposes, and how we are to live and relate to other people. The Bible contains wisdom for life, but also, through a mysterious process that I do not fully understand, it serves as spiritual food that strengthens us in our spiritual resolve. It helps us not only to know the will of God but to choose and do it, even when there are impulses within us that pull us in another direction. The following passages tell us something of how the Word of God works in our lives.

Psalms 119:105: "Your word is a lamp to my feet, and a light to my path."

Psalm 119:11: "Your word have I hidden in my heart, that I might not sin against You."

Matthew 4:4: "But He answered and said, "It is written, 'Man shall not live by bread alone, but by every word that proceeds from the mouth of God.'"

Romans 10:17: "So then faith comes by hearing, and hearing by the word of God."

Paul said in Ephesians 6:17 that the Word of God is the sword of the Holy Spirit. The Word of God is essential to our spiritual life, and if we neglect it, that will be to our great peril. If you do not teach it to your children and teach them to study it, meditate on it, and teach it to their children, you will do them great harm.

Prayer is Essential to Being Right and Living Right

Prayer is talking with God. The Holy Bible admonishes us to "pray without ceasing (1 Thessalonians 5:17)." To pray without ceasing does not mean we should never do anything but pray; it means whatever we are doing we should consciously maintain our hearts (or minds) in an attitude of openness before God, desiring His direction to enable us to know and do what is best, and very frequently praising Him and asking His specific direction and help with our current activities.

Our praying should not be a perfunctory form. It should involve self-examination, repentance, confession, worship, and petition for ourselves and for others, for Christ's work in and through the Church, for the glory of God to be demonstrated in our lives and in all creation, and for so many other things I can't possibly name them. We need to pray specific petitions for ourselves and others whom we know, not "broad brush" generalities. We should always be desiring and seeking God's will, not our own, in our praying—not an easy thing to do. The biblical passages that speak of prayer and other spiritual disciplines are far too numerous to mention, but what is commonly called "the Lord's Prayer," in which Jesus taught His disciples to pray, and Psalm 23 are good models for us. (See also John 17 for an example of our Lord praying His own prayer to the Father). We are not to recite them only but to analyze them and pray concerning the categories of issues that our Lord mentioned. It would be well worth your while to read the Valley of Vision, a book of Puritans' prayers, and also anything on prayer written by Charles Spurgeon and/or A. W. Tozer.

Living in the Family of God

Regular attendance to the means of grace with other believers in Christ in a local church that follows a biblical model is commanded by the Word of God. Quickly seek out a church and go to worship regularly, wherever you go. We are commanded to assemble and join ourselves together with other believers in the worship and service of God, another of the essential spiritual disciplines (Hebrews 10:25). There is nothing in the Bible to support the idea that one can be a Christian and follow and please Christ in chosen isolation from other believers, when there are other believers around with whom one can worship and share life.

Congregating with other believers in Christ to worship God and building relationships with them is not optional for a Christian. The Church is a body, the spiritual body of Christ inhabited by the Holy Spirit. It is a spiritual family comprised of many local congregations all of whom should be autonomous but interdependent. The church is not a building nor a human religious organization. To ignore or reject the body of Christ or the family of God is unnatural, unhealthy, and proud, arrogant defiance of the Word of God. Most Sundays should find us gathered with other Christians, worshiping our Lord and hearing His Word.

It is through our relationships with others, both the pleasant relationships and the difficult ones, that Christ works in us to develop His character, make us all more like Him, and show Himself to the world. We need others; they need us.

There are people who would tell you these things are legalism, but they are not. Legalism is doing things in the hope of justifying and thus saving oneself. Loving obedience to Christ is the result of the gracious work of His Spirit within us (Ephesians 2:10). There will be times when you will tire, not seeing how you are benefiting, and will tell yourself this is just a religious ritual, but it is more. It is similar to running: without pain, there is no gain. We are in a spiritual pilgrimage through this life, and these disciplines will sustain you when the way is difficult and will help you finish the race victoriously. They are commanded by the Word of God, and to do contrary is disobedience, will inevitably have negative consequences for those who do not practice them, and will leave their children without the precious spiritual, moral, and ethical heritage that they themselves may have had.

Fasting and Practicing Self-control

Fasting is choosing to go without food for a specific period of time and for a purpose. The word breakfast means to break, or end, the (overnight) fast. In Spanish the word is desayuno and means the same thing. Some people have the idea that they should fast to get God to do something they desire. That is an error. If God has (in eternity past) determined to do (or not do) something, no one can compel or persuade Him to a contrary course.

I know of no Scriptures that command fasting but several that appear to assume that the follower in Christ will do so. They begin, "When you fast, etc." or similarly. As best I can determine, fasting seems to have a couple of purposes. One is described in Isaiah 58:1–11. The Lord said through the prophet, "Is this not the fast that I have chosen: to loose the bonds of wickedness, to undo the heavy burdens, to let the oppressed go free, and that you break every yoke? Is it not to share your bread with the hungry, and that you bring to your house the poor who are cast out; when you see the naked, that you cover him, and not hide yourself from your own flesh (Isaiah 58:6, 7)?" I understand that to mean that one chooses to profit less from his employees so that he can pay them more, or that we eat less ourselves so we can share the bounty God has given us with those who are in need. This is not very mystical but a very practical demonstration of God's kindness to others. Christ commanded us to give to those who ask of us.

Our Lord seems to allude to another function of fasting when He was teaching His apostles why they had been unable to help a demon possessed lad and told them, "However, this kind [of demon] does not go out except by prayer and fasting (Matthew 17:21)." I think the issue here was not that they could by prayer and fasting persuade God to grant them power to expel the demon. I believe it is that through prayer we have intercourse with God, and through fasting we deny our temporal, physical desires the ability to control us so that we can focus more on spiritual and eternal matters, drawing nearer to God (2 Corinthians 4:18). Then, when we draw nearer to God, we will better understand His purposes and there are fewer inconsistent things in us to impede His Spirit from working through us. Self-control is one of the fruits of the Spirit listed in Galatians 5:22, 23, and fasting is probably necessary to develop it to a significant degree. I have probably done more poorly at this than any other of the spiritual disciplines. Everything in our contemporary world is opposed to it, and we must stand against the current to practice fasting.

"But solid food belongs to those who are of full age, that is, those who by reason of use have their senses exercised to discern both good and evil (Hebrews 5:14)."

Loving through Giving

"So let each one give as he purposes in his heart, not grudgingly or of necessity; for God loves a cheerful giver (2 Corinthians 9:7)." The Bible talks quite a lot about the selfishness that is an inherent part of the nature of every person and even more so before being regenerated by the Spirit of God. When that occurs, one is made a child of God (John 1:11–13), and the Holy Spirit starts changing him to make him more and more like our Lord. God is love (1 John 4:7, 8), and He expresses His love to us by giving us good things, especially His Word, His Son Who is the incarnate Word, but also every good thing we receive is a gift of God to us (James 1:17).

God does not need us, but He chooses to pour out on us His undeserved favor. Of all the changes God makes in us (2 Corinthians 5:17), I doubt any are more indicative of a genuine work of grace than when we begin to think more about the well-being of others and put others ahead of ourselves. That is especially seen in generosity, as we delight to share the good things God has granted us with others. "And hope makes not ashamed; because the love of God is shed abroad in our hearts by the Holy Spirit which is given unto us (Romans 5:5, my paraphrase)."

57

We are commanded to support the work of the church and ministry and told that "Pure and undefiled religion before God and the Father is this: to visit orphans and widows in their trouble, and to keep oneself unspotted from the world (James 1:27)." Christ said the poor will always be with us, and they need our help, but we need to help even more so. The apostle Paul reminded the elders at Ephesus, "I have shown you in every way, by laboring like this, that you must support the weak. And remember the words of the Lord Jesus, that He said, 'It is more blessed to give than to receive (Acts 20:35).'" Never give so that you will be blessed; that is not love and generosity but greed and hypocrisy. But be sure of this: God is no man's debtor; one cannot "outgive" God. When we leave here, we will leave all our material possessions behind, so let's be sure that we use them well and for eternity while we can.

Evangelism

Evangelism simply means talking with other people, especially those who don't know Christ, about the good news of what God has done in Christ to bring us pardon for sin and eternal life. (Evangelio is the Spanish word for "gospel, the good news." It is very similar in Latin and Greek.) Christ made it very clear that this is the responsibility of all who believe in and follow Him. He said, "Go therefore and make disciples of all the nations, baptizing them in the name of the Father and of the Son and of the Holy Spirit, teaching

58

them to observe all things that I have commanded you; and lo, I am with you always, even to the end of the age (Matthew 28:19, 20)." That is called the Great Commission. It is a command Christ gave to His followers before He ascended into heaven. He stated it in such a manner that it is clearly a perpetual command for all Christians in every age and place.

Similarly, He said, "But you shall receive power when the Holy Spirit has come upon you; and you shall be witnesses of Me in Jerusalem, and in all Judea and Samaria, and to the end of the earth (Acts 1:8, my paraphrase)." The Holy Spirit made it clear through the apostle Paul in Romans 10 (and other passages) that it is through hearing the gospel that He brings sinners to repentance, faith in Christ, and eternal life. That is the way we came to be children of God (John 1:11–13), and having been so blessed we have the obligation to extend that same lifeline to others who need to be saved just as we did. Many people seem to think that is the responsibility only of pastors and others in religious vocations, but that is false! We all have that responsibility—even though it may not be easy for us to tell others of Christ and may sometimes provoke rejection and ridicule, we must be obedient to our Lord to have His approval and blessing. If we do not do so, then we will bear the guilt for those who were eternally lost and whom we failed to warn (Ezekiel 33:8).

One may evangelize by preaching God's Word to a church from the pulpit, by teaching a Sunday School class, by going to visit those in hospitals, nursing homes, prisons, and jails (Matthew 25:31–46), by handing someone a gospel pamphlet or book, by talking to a neighbor or friend, by canvassing the homes in a subdivision and asking the residents about their relationship with Christ and inviting them to study the Bible. Or as Caraleen and I did, one may go to live in another country where people are not encouraged to read the Bible and teach them the gospel. How and where we do it is not nearly so important, but it is absolutely imperative that we do it! When one becomes accustomed to sharing the gospel anywhere outside of a religious environment, then it becomes easier to do it everywhere. Are you a follower of Christ? Are you obeying Christ by telling others about Him?

Now let's look at some other specific biblical values, principles, and commandments that should guide us in how we live. We should apply ourselves to make sure the following characteristics are an integral part of our character and regularly seen in our behavior.

Biblical Values to Guide Us:
Becoming and Living Like Jesus

Love, Altruism, and Generosity

There are several kinds of love, including the love for parents, children, and siblings, as well as the erotic love for a spouse. But the kind we are concerned with here is the kind of love God has and gives to us that, without regard to merit, fixes affection on others and seeks their well-being even ahead of our own. Altruism is delighting in helping someone else, doing good because it is good, because sometimes people need help and we can help. It is the opposite of hedonism, just doing what one feels like doing without regard for how it affects others. One might love another without their awareness, but kindness and generosity makes that love apparent. Generosity is caring about others and helping them by sharing our resources with them, whether time, talent, or material resources (things that can be purchased).

A man named Benjamin who was president of the teachers' union in Guanajuato, who along with his wife Virginia, studied with us asked me several years ago how a person can find (enduring) happiness. I told him the way to find happiness is by learning to delight in helping others. There are many people around us who need help, and so there are many opportunities to find happiness by helping. This is one of many important truths (values, attitudes) that one does not just instinctively know but that is acquired by experience, by a desire to learn, and by the work of the Holy Spirit who puts His love within us.

Naturally, people are acquisitive, tend to compete with others, and hoard resources for themselves. I think it is rare that one is really generous with others until God has done a transforming work in them, and I believe generosity is one of the clearest indications of a really spiritual Christian character, demonstrating the kind of unconditional love God has for us. When we have good and right attitudes and do well, we should never attribute that to ourselves and believe it is because we are better than someone else. We should instead realize it is because God has had mercy on us to keep us from evil (Matthew 6:13) and to put within us something of His own mind and heart.

People, including Christians, often believe God is directing them in something when it is only their imagination or their proud and selfish motives. The one time we can know we are being directed by God is when we are doing that which is right and good as it is indicated in His Word, the Bible, although even then we can do it for the wrong motives (e.g., to show others how good and religious we are, etc.). We should examine our motives but always do what we know is right, and if we suspect our own motives, we should repent but still do what is right (1 John 3:4, 5:17; James 4:17).

I do not believe that anyone just naturally delights in helping (serving) others because we are all born with a selfish nature and our first interest in relating to others is in seeing how we may gain from them what we need and/or want. We do need others. There are things others can do for us that we cannot do for ourselves, and God made us to be social beings that enjoy the company of others, and there is nothing wrong with that. The problem is when our focus is almost exclusively on ourselves and we fail to respect and value others, fail to be concerned with their well-being, and fail to recognize or care how our behavior can harm them. When that happens, in our effort to protect ourselves and exploit others for our own perceived benefit, we alienate them and cut ourselves off from the acceptance, inclusion, and affection (love) that we need and that is essential to enduring happiness.

When one is selfish, he or she is the opposite of God who cares for us and gave His Son for us, without anything in us to deserve it, when He did not need us and was absolutely complete without us. Because we all need friends and at various times need their help, no one has too many friends. There are always people around us who need a friend and some who feel rejected and alone.

If we choose to, you and I can be friends to someone who needs a friend rather than seeking the acceptance of the popular or powerful person whom we might think could help us but who is sought by many others for the same reason and who may care about no one but himself. "A man who has friends must himself be friendly, but there is a friend who sticks closer than a brother (Proverbs 18:24)." When one shows that he is a faithful and caring friend, his or her friendship will usually be appreciated with the result that he will not only be a friend but will have many friends and enjoy all the benefits of those friendships. "When a man's ways please the LORD, He makes even his enemies to be at peace with him (Proverbs 16:7)." I think that means he will be the kind of person others will want for a friend or even an employee. However, one should recognize that the proverbs are general principles about human relationships; they are not assertions that things will work this way in every instance.

One will never find happiness in this way if his "friendship" to another is feigned and only for the purpose of accruing benefits to himself. Power, possessions, and adulation may succeed in bringing one temporary satisfaction, but it will not endure in the absence of rewarding, caring, relationships with other people. But there is a problem: I said above that no one naturally delights in serving other people because we come into this world with a twisted selfish nature. The only way that we can delight in serving others and not for anything we hope to gain is if and when God, our Creator, with His Spirit, makes a change in us and puts within us His own unconditional love so that we may share it with others. We should ask Him frequently to do that.

"And hope makes not ashamed; because the love of God is shed abroad in our hearts by the Holy Spirit which is given unto us (Romans 5:5, KJV)." That is the new spiritual birth spoken of in John 1:13, 3:3; II Corinthians 5:17; 1 Peter 1:3, 23; and Ephesians 2:1, 5. Christ said to Nicodemus, "You must be born again (Jn. 3:1-8)," but He did not tell him anything he could do to bring that about, and that is because we cannot do anything to bring about our own birth, either natural or spiritual; it is something that only God does. If we understand that, it will humble us and cause us unceasing gratitude to the Holy and infinite God who has chosen and loved an unworthy sinner. If you desire that new spiritual nature (similar to that of Christ) that only God can give but are anxious that you cannot achieve it by your own will, you should talk to God about that, confessing your sins to Him and asking Him to forgive you because Christ suffered for the sins of those who will trust in Him. If you really desire to be pleasing to God and live a righteous life it is almost certainly because He has put that desire within you and may very well have already given you the new birth. Just do not assume that without seeing biblical evidences in your life to confirm it.

When God sovereignly and arbitrarily invades our life and changes our values, perspectives, and purposes in living, then we can begin to find joy in being a real friend and helping others (Romans 3:10, 11; Ephesians 2:1, 5). I hope you will realize that things are to be used and enjoyed, but only God and people, whom He made in many respects similar to Himself, are to be loved. As we get nearer the end of our terrestrial pilgrimage, we become more acutely aware that we will leave behind everything we have accumulated and we will wish we had invested more of our time, effort, and resources in loving, helping, and enjoying other people. Do it while there is time and opportunity, and avoid the

sorrow and regret that would otherwise come.

Kindness, Gentleness, and Mercy

Kindness is much like altruism. Altruism is completely, unselfishly seeking the well-being of another. Kindness and gentleness are, in the same way, being aware of how our behavior may help or injure others, and deliberately and consistently choosing to help rather than hurt others. One may be kind to another by actively doing something the other will enjoy or from which he or she will benefit. Another way of being kind is to think before acting (or speaking) and avoid that which will harm or humiliate another. To show mercy is to be kind in some way or help another for no reason but that the other has a need and God has granted us the ability to help.

"And be kind to one another, tenderhearted, forgiving one another, just as God in Christ forgave you (Ephesians 4:32)."

"And whoever gives one of these little ones only a cup of cold water in the name of a disciple, assuredly, I say to you, he shall by no means lose his reward (Matthew 10:42)."

"Blessed is he who considers the poor; the LORD will deliver him in time of trouble. The LORD will preserve him and keep him alive, and he will be blessed on the earth; You will not deliver him to the will of his enemies. The LORD will strengthen him on his bed of illness; You will sustain him on his sickbed (Psalm 41:1–3)."

Holiness, Moral Purity

The Bible says that God is holy and we are to be holy (1 Peter 1:16). It also uses the term "sanctify" and that means to make something or someone holy. To be holy means to be clean or pure and good, and by that difference separated or distinguished from everything that is not right, moral, pure, and good.

Sometimes, because we are finite and therefore incapable of understanding the mysterious and infinite providence that directs all of the complex variables of God's universe and impinge on our lives, we ask the "why" question without even realizing that we are implying things might have been, perhaps should have been, done differently and better. When we do that, we are ignoring all that the Bible has revealed to us about God: He is the personification of kindness, righteousness, wisdom, knowledge, and power. "And we know that all things work together for good to those who love God, to those who are the called according to His purpose (Romans 8:28)." Any idea of God that is not consistent with the character of God that is clearly proclaimed in the Bible is wrong and should be immediately rejected.

There are terrible consequences that continue to occur as the result of our first parents believing the serpent who only comes to steal, kill, and destroy (John 10:10) rather than trusting their Creator who had given them a perfect environment. Among the many things we don't know is why God has chosen to take thousands of years to "destroy the works of the devil (1 John 3:8)" and erase the impact of unbelief/sin on humanity and the rest of creation. I don't know whether we will ever have the answers to all our questions, but I do know that much more important than having those answers is learning to trust God, to know that He is absolutely Good, and He always does absolutely the best of all possibilities in the lives of His people. God is holy and He is making us like Himself (Romans 8:29). Let that reassure your mind and heart when you are hurting, sorrowing, and perplexed; remember that "the LORD God, the God of Israel, only does wondrous things (Psalm 72:18)."

I deliberately placed the discussion of purity and morality after our discussion of love because in our culture sometimes sexual activity is confused with love. Sexual relationships are intended by God as a means to procreation (having children) and also as a very intimate way of expressing our love to our husband or wife. But it is only within marriage that it is pure and good. "For from within, out of the heart of men, proceed evil thoughts, adulteries, fornications, murders, thefts, covetousness, wickedness, deceit, lewdness, an evil eye, blasphemy, pride, foolishness. All these evil things come from within and defile a man (Mark 7:21–23)."

The Bible calls behavior outside of marriage that deliberately excites sexual passions lasciviousness (lewdness) and concupiscence (evil desire) and calls sexual intercourse outside of marriage fornication (sexual immorality) and/or adultery. All of that is to say that sexual activity is to be reserved for marriage and any behavior that specifically stimulates a heightened awareness of, and desire for, sexual activity (if it is not between a husband and wife) is not love; it is evil in God's eyes and is condemned and will be judged by Him. Men and women are naturally attracted to one another, and that attraction is not wrong. It is wrong if we fail to control those impulses, if we encourage and/or gratify them outside of the committed marriage relationship, contrary to the commands of God. It is very important that we are aware of our ability to excite one another and that we do not use that ability to attract and control another person.

We are to maintain the purity of our bodies as temples of the Holy Spirit (1 Corinthians 3:16, 6:19), observe the boundaries the Bible gives us in our relationships, and be careful not to provoke another person to evil desire and/or behavior. It is not only in sexuality that we are to exemplify morality and be distinguished as people who really love God and love our neighbor, but we are to do so in all of our conduct. When we are honest, ethical, and compassionate in our interaction with others and embrace and practice the values that we are discussing here, we are choosing to separate ourselves unto God in distinction from those who reject him. "Great peace have those who love Your law, and nothing causes them to stumble (Psalm 119:165)." The subject of holiness deserves a lengthier treatment, but it is beyond the scope of this book. See Holiness by J. C. Ryle for a thorough discussion.

Truthfulness

Jesus said, "I am the Way, the Truth, and the Life (John 14:6)." Truthfulness is fundamental to Christianity and simply to being an honest person of integrity. "You shall not bear false witness against your neighbor (Exodus 20:16)," one of the Ten Commandments, prohibits being untruthful/dishonest in the specific case of making a false allegation about another person and their behavior. Being truthful eliminates that specious behavior but also has a much broader application (Colossians 3:9). It will prevent us from representing ourselves falsely to impress another or gain advantage. We commonly despise it in another but often find it very inconvenient and difficult for ourselves to consistently be truthful. Deceit is a characteristic of the enemy. In Scripture he is called the father of lies. It was through lies and misrepresentation that he seduced our first parents into doubting the kindness, faithfulness, and truthfulness of the Creator and Sustainer of the universe, rebelling and disobeying God, and thus bequeathing to all their progeny a sinful, selfish, fearful, depraved nature.

Could you imagine God being other than truthful, the One upon whom all life, existence, and reality depends? God identified himself as the I AM (Exodus 3:14), the ground of being, the self-existent One who is the source of all else. I think perhaps that is why truthfulness is so important: without knowing the truth (i.e., what is real; John 8:31, 32), nothing is certain, and the world is a terrifying place that I do not want to imagine and in which I would not want to live. It is the frightening world of some people with mental illnesses.

Honesty, Fairness, and Justice

Honesty requires one to be truthful in his or her statements, but it also requires the absence of any deceit and assuring that we are completely scrupulous with others in all our interactions. We are to be just, "fair" in our dealings with others, treating others as we want to be treated, not taking advantage of them, and we are to seek justice for others in our society and before the law. The desire and intent to express mercy and kindness can never serve as an adequate basis for condoning injustice because if we do so, we become complicit in victimizing those who have been treated unjustly. Only when we are the person who has been treated unfairly do we have the discretion to forego the demand for justice in favor of granting mercy, and even then we must be careful to avoid by our leniency encouraging further manipulation and exploitation from which all society suffers. There are many scriptures in the Old Testament and the New Testament that forbid theft, that command just weights and balances, and require justice in paying wages and working diligently to earn them. "Therefore, whatever you want men to do to you, do also to them, for this is the Law and the Prophets (Matthew 7:12)."

"LORD, who may abide in Your tabernacle? Who may dwell in Your holy hill? He who walks uprightly, and works righteousness, and speaks the truth in his heart; he who does not backbite with his tongue, nor does evil to his neighbor, nor does he take up a reproach against his friend; in whose eyes a vile person is despised, but he honors those who fear the LORD; he who swears to his own hurt and does not change; he who does not put out his money at usury, nor does he take a bribe against the innocent. He who does these things shall never be moved (Psalm 15)."

Faith, Trust, Hope

Trust is a better word than belief to express what the Bible is speaking of when it tells us we are to believe in God and specifically in Christ, and that those who are justified by Christ live by faith. That is, faith or trust is the guiding principle of their lives, and in consequence of that trust in Christ (that God has formed in them— Ephesians 2:8–10) they receive God's undeserved favor and will continue to live forever (Romans 1:17). We are to be wise, not gullible, people, and we are not to trust those who are manifestly untrustworthy and who will do us great harm if given the chance. But we are to trust God always, who never fails to perform His Word and demonstrate His kind and gracious character.

Further, to build trust relationships, someone has to be the first to become vulnerable, to take a chance and let down his guard, hoping that other Christian brethren and people who appear as persons of integrity will reciprocate. Nobody should be more prepared to do so than the person who knows that Christ exposed Himself to suffering and death for us who have transgressed against the Father, to win us and bring us back to Him.

Many people think they have trusted in Christ and/or do trust Him, when in fact they have not and do not. Let's consider what it means to trust in Christ. It does not mean that a person can receive God's eternal salvation by simply saying he trusts in Christ when the same person wants nothing more to do with Christ other than to escape the punishment for his sins and gives no evidence of trusting in Christ by following Him.

When the Bible talks of "believing in" or "trusting in" Christ, that means having confidence that He is who He said He is, the eternal Son of God; that everything He said is true and He will do what He said; that through His death on the cross He paid for the sins of those that trust in Him; that He has the right to our affection and obedience; and that following Him will produce the best possible result for us. That kind of faith in Christ will inevitably cause us to obey Him—not perfectly every minute of our lives because we are not perfect—but obedience to Christ will be the characteristic of our lives rather than unbelief, rebellion, greed, deceit, immorality, and disobedience. The Bible is very clear that it is only people who trust and follow Christ that will spend eternity with Christ. Others will be separated from Him in unending torment.

"Believe on the Lord Jesus Christ, and you will be saved (Acts 16:31)."

"Trust in the LORD with all your heart, and lean not on your own understanding; in all your ways acknowledge Him, and He shall direct your paths (Proverbs 3:5)."

"Repent ye therefore, and be converted, that your sins may be blotted out, when the times of refreshing shall come from the presence of the Lord (Acts 3:19, KJV)."

Respect, Courtesy, and Honor (to Whom Honor Is Due—Romans 13:7)

Someone has said courtesy is the oil that lubricates the machinery of human relationships (and keeps it running smoothly). I have counseled with many couples who were having conflict in their marriages and many who were on the verge of divorce, and I doubt that in any of them both parties (oftentimes neither) regularly treated his/her spouse with the courtesy and respect that we should show even to an associate in the school, at work, or to a stranger. The Bible says "A soft answer turns away wrath, but a harsh word stirs up anger (Proverbs 15:1);" "A man who has friends must himself be friendly, but there is a friend who sticks closer than a brother (Proverbs 18:24);" and "Therefore, whatever you want men to do to you, do also to them, for this is the Law and the Prophets (Matthew 7:12)." If all spouses were to obey those three verses, I doubt there would ever be divorces.

We are to treat others with kindness and respect because they and we are equally creatures made by God, and in some respects similar to Him. We are not better than others nor do we deserve better than they, so we ought to treat them as we desire to be treated. It is especially important that we demonstrate this to our children, teach it to them, and require it of them. We should permit reasonable questions and discussion but not persistent "talking-back," never profanity or name-calling, sullenness, stomping, or door-slamming as a show of angry resentment. We should not permit those things in our children and certainly not do them ourselves. If we respect and honor those around us, it will produce more profitable and enjoyable interaction for others and for us.

"Where do wars and fights come from among you? Do they not come from your desires for pleasure that war in your members? You lust and do not have. You murder and covet and cannot obtain. You fight and war. Yet you do not have because you do not ask. You ask and do not receive, because you ask amiss, that you may spend it on your pleasures (James 4:1–3)." This "asking" might include asking God in prayer, but I believe it also applies to requesting the help and cooperation of others, without attempting to compel it, and while recognizing the other's autonomy and right to refuse. Most of our relationships are voluntary; there is very little we can actually force another to do. So, we need to learn to respect others, engage and serve them, and win their collaboration while giving our own. "And be kind to one another, tenderhearted, forgiving one another, just as God in Christ forgave you (Ephesians 4:32)." Do not misunderstand me: I am speaking of equals here, not of parents and their children and the necessity for parents to require respect and obedience of their children and to discipline them when necessary to secure their obedience.

I doubt that we are ever really unhappy with someone else except when they are not doing what we wish. That is to say, we have been unable to control them (although we normally don't admit that is what we try to do). The capacity to control others belongs to God, not to us, and we will never be happy so long as we insist on trying to do what we cannot possibly do. "God grant me the serenity to accept the things I cannot change, the courage to change the things I can [that should be changed], and the wisdom to know the difference. Amen." (attributed to Reinhold Niebuhr)

Gratitude, Thankfulness

Good parents who love their children want good things for them, and it is common for them to think they want their children to enjoy better conditions than they have had themselves. That may result in parents indulging their children, giving them almost everything they want, while failing to give them responsibility and teaching them to work. As a result, such children will likely have a sense of entitlement, be selfish, arrogant, and lacking in compassion for others. When the world does not indulge such a person like the parents have, they become angry, abusive, and may even attempt or commit suicide. All this indicates that parents should be careful not to give their children so much that everything loses its value. Material things can only give us momentary diversion; they cannot confer lasting happiness. One can have lasting happiness when he learns to find it in serving others. There is no lack of opportunity for that, and the person who does so will usually find many who seek his company.

We should learn that we are not more deserving than others and that we have the things we have not because we are especially deserving but because there are people who love us and want us to be well and happy, and because God has caused us to be born with good health and in fortuitous circumstances. Consequently, one should not be over-indulged, children should be disciplined when needed to learn to respect others and to adopt moral and honorable behavior, and they should be taught and learn gratitude (thankfulness)—gratitude first of all to God, and then to those around them who have blessed their lives. I believe that will also help one learn to be more generous in sharing those things with which God has blessed us.

"Every good gift and every perfect gift is from above, and comes down from the Father of lights, with whom there is no variation or shadow of turning (James 1:17)."

"For we brought nothing into this world, and it is certain we can carry nothing out (1 Timothy 6:7)."

"In everything give thanks; for this is the will of God in Christ Jesus concerning you (1 Thessalonians 5:18)."

Contentment

"Not that I speak in regard to need, for I have learned in whatever state I am, to be content: I know how to be abased, and I know how to abound. Everywhere and in all things I have learned both to be full and to be hungry, both to abound and to suffer need. I can do all things through Christ Who strengthens me." So said the apostle Paul in Philippians 4:11–13. Contentment can be learned, acquired; it is not the common condition of mankind. People are usually unsatisfied, except for brief intervals, and then they are seeking something more. That is because we have been alienated, separated from God; we will never have enduring happiness until we find it in Him.

God created a marvelous environment in which we live and He made us with the capacity to enjoy it. Because we enjoy life, we can become addicted to pleasant experiences and begin to live primarily for that stimulation. If we do so, we will be on an endless search for something to satisfy us because all pleasure is only momentary, and we will then miss the purpose of our existence and the greatest joy and satisfaction that we could ever know. God did not intend that we should be absorbed by the gifts and experiences He gives us; He made us above all to know and glorify Him, and to enjoy Him forever. (Westminster Shorter Catechism)

After loving God, we are to love those around us. We are to love people and use things, not the reverse. When we learn to do that, we know the joy of what the Bible calls koinonia or "fellowship." After just a few years of mortal life, we will leave behind all the things we have spent a lifetime acquiring, and all we will retain is Christ and the loving relationships we have gained by loving others (see Ecclesiastes).

God is so far superior to us that we can never even get close to understanding why He has ordained many of the individual details of our lives and our world (Isaiah 55:8, 9). Some people who insist on having all the answers lose their faith in God because they assume that if they do not understand, then there must be no good reason. Instead, we need to learn when we are confronted with difficult circumstances, after we have made good use of the intelligence God has given us and still have no good explanation, to simply bow before Him and trust Him, knowing He has good reason for all He does, and He always does the best for those who belong to Him. "The secret things belong to the LORD our God, but those things which are revealed belong to us and to our children forever, that we may do all the words of this law (Deuteronomy 29:29)."

Only after Christ comes and establishes His kingdom on the earth and does away with all trace of sin will pain, sorrow, death, and confusion be eliminated. Until then, if we look to Christ and trust Him, we can learn to be content in riches or poverty, in sickness or in health, and that is much better than becoming bitter over things we do not like and cannot control. If you read Of the Imitation of Christ by Thomas á Kempis and The Rare Jewel of Christian Contentment by Jeremiah Burroughs, they may help you better understand and deal with these things.

"Do not love the world or the things in the world. If anyone loves the world, the love of the Father is not in him. For all that is in the world—the lust of the flesh, the lust of the eyes, and the pride of life—is not of the Father but is of the world (1 John 2:15, 16)."

Industry (the Disposition to Work: Ethic and Practice)

The Bible has a lot to say about work.

"Then the LORD God took the man and put him in the garden of Eden to tend and keep it (Genesis 2:15)."

"Therefore the LORD God sent him out of the garden of Eden to till the ground from which he was taken (Genesis 3:23)."

"Let him who stole steal no longer, but rather let him labor, working with his hands what is good, that he may have something to give him who has need (Ephesians 4:28)." "For even when we were with you, we commanded you this: If anyone will not work, neither shall he eat (II Thessalonians 3:10)."

"But if anyone does not provide for his own, and especially for those of his household, he has denied the faith and is worse than an unbeliever (1 Timothy 5:8)."

The Bible teaches that industry, or work, is the responsibility of mankind and that it is a virtue. That idea, growing out of the Bible and given new impetus in the Protestant Reformation, has been widely believed in past decades to be responsible for the great economic and technological prosperity of Europe and the United States as compared with other underdeveloped countries. It is important that we learn to work and take satisfaction in the opportunity and ability to work so that we can take care of our own needs and the needs of our family first of all. Having done that, we are to have compassion on others who have legitimate needs for which they cannot provide—people like widows, orphans, the elderly, and the infirm. Our Lord even said, "Give to him who asks you, and from him who wants to borrow from you do not turn away (Matthew 5:42)." That is not always easy for us to do, and a careful explication of the matter is beyond the scope of our task here, but I must say we don't want to encourage laziness and indigence, on the one hand, nor on the other hand let that concern become an excuse for a lack of generosity and obedience to Christ in this matter.

To provide for our own needs or those of anyone else there are only two options: work and theft (deceit, robbery). So, it is important that we accept our responsibilities and learn to work and to enjoy working so we can have the resources to do things that are worthwhile. It is equally important that we teach our children and require them to work. Give responsibilities to your children; find worthwhile things for them to do and require them to do them well. To fail in this is negligence and will harm them and make them a plague to the society in which they live. While we are working, we are exercising our bodies and our minds and gaining health benefits in doing so. "He who is slothful in his work is a brother to him who is a great destroyer (Proverbs 18:9)."

Self-control, Self-discipline

Self-control is also one of the fruits of the Holy Spirit (Galatians 5:22, 23), so we might think of it not so much as self-control but as being under the control of God's Spirit and doing what is pleasing to Him. I think it is called self-control because one is not conscious of any compulsion, by the Holy Spirit or anyone else, and because it is a matter of controlling one's behavior and not yielding quickly to impulses that might prove rash. The person who is exercising self-control is not impulsive, reacting to circumstances emotionally, but is instead thinking carefully, evaluating each situation, and making decisions about his behavior based on his understanding of God's Word and will, and what might be the consequences of his actions.

Most people with whom I have counseled who were having conflict with others, whether spouse, child, parent, employee, employer, or neighbor, etc., were not making careful decisions guided by God's Word. In fact, one may often do things that, had he taken time to think carefully, he could have anticipated the words or behavior would produce a reaction and situation that he would not like. But he/she was behaving emotionally and impulsively, not rationally, kindly, and compassionately. A person who is self-disciplined will almost certainly have predetermined structure, or moral and ethical boundaries, he or she has chosen to guide his behavior so that he or she will not frequently be surprised by events that occur and, caught unawares, make rash decisions. May we be guided by wisdom, our knowledge of God's Word, and our understanding of human needs and behavior, not ruled by our emotions.

"A soft answer turns away wrath, but a harsh word stirs up anger (Proverbs 15:1)."

"Whoever has no rule over his own spirit is like a city broken down, without walls (Proverbs 25:28)."

"A brother offended is harder to win than a strong city, and contentions are like the bars of a castle (Proverbs 18:19)."

Childrearing and Discipline

"Children are a heritage from the LORD," says Psalm 127:3. They are a blessing from the Lord that can bring us great happiness, but parents also have a great responsibility for the care and training of their children. That responsibility cannot be delegated to anyone else. Parents will give account to God for how they perform this task. It begins with providing nourishment, affection, clothing, shelter, protection, and then training.

Children must be protected from harm and warned of dangers. As soon as they are able to begin to comprehend, as early as the age of two or three, spiritual training should begin, teaching the child about God, the Bible, and prayer, what God wants from us, being part of a local biblical church, how one is to relate to others, and continuing to cover all the issues we are discussing in this discourse. Children must be taught courtesy, to respect and honor others; God, their parents, other adults, their peers, and all who show themselves worthy of honor. They must be given appropriate tasks like personal hygiene, cleaning their room, and other tasks around the home and required to perform them. In doing so, children will learn to find satisfaction in doing work that is good and necessary rather than expecting to be idle, granted all their wishes, and expecting others will do the difficult and unpleasant tasks for them. A Jewish proverb says, "A man will teach his son to work, or teach him to be a thief." These are the only two options.

In addition to simply learning to work, children and youth must be taught how to perform specific tasks that require knowledge and skill. They must learn how to communicate with others face-to-face, electronically, and in written form. They need to learn how to mow the lawn, to cook, launder clothing, tell time, count money, how to open a bank account and balance the statement, how to ride a bicycle, drive a car, perform basic maintenance tasks on an auto, how to safely and effectively use and care for a firearm. They need to learn about the history and institutions of our republic, to value our freedoms, and to vote. They need to learn to dress appropriately for various circumstances, about relating properly to the opposite sex, what to look for in choosing a spouse, and how to love and care for their spouse and children. Only when children are trained well is it then appropriate to administer discipline as needed to encourage correct behavior. "For whom the

LORD loves He chastens, and scourges every son whom He receives. If you endure chastening, God deals with you as with sons; for what son is there whom a father does not chasten (Hebrews 12:6, 7)?"

The purpose of discipline is to induce repentance and therefore a change from wrong behavior. God disciplines his children for that purpose and at times the church must discipline wayward members for their benefit. God does this because He is holy and because He loves us, and the Church imposes discipline because we love others, especially our brethren, and our conduct should reflect the glory of God. When discipline is most effective it will aid us to internalize the values and standards of behavior that God has given us so that we will develop self-discipline, desiring to live a godly life and becoming progressively more like Christ. Parents who have not learned self-discipline cannot be most effective at training their children.

Children must be disciplined to learn to exercise self-discipline, engage in socially acceptable behavior, and avoid developing an anti-social personality. A child should be thoroughly taught about expected conduct and never disciplined without having been previously instructed about rules for behavior. Neither should parents discipline a child when the parent is angry and perhaps venting his anger instead of seeking the child's correction and well-being. The purpose of discipline is to produce repentance, a "change of mind," about wrong behavior. It is a good idea to remind the child clearly and calmly of the rule for behavior that he or she has chosen to violate and pray with him or her prior to administering discipline.

I believe there are three categories of offenses that include every reason for discipline: **defiance, malice, and negligence**.

Defiance includes disobedience but can also be the blatant rejection of authority (that has been established by God), even without specific disobedience, and it should not be tolerated. Defiance can be seen in disrespectful language, scowling, stomping, and slamming doors in anger, and these things should not be tolerated. Parents should not demean their children; they should speak to them with love and respect, and require the same of them. The epistle of James says a great deal about the tongue and the harm it can cause. We should read and discuss it periodically with our children and make a big deal of the speech that we and they use, commending the good and reproving that which is harmful.

Malice is the deliberate intent to do harm to another and is demonstrated by speech and/or other potentially harmful behavior.

Negligence is behavior that is careless of the risk of harm to others. There should be discipline appropriate to the magnitude of the offense for each of these behaviors. Be sure not to use your big disciplinary "guns" for small offenses and then have nothing more to use if the occasion comes when there has been a really big offense and you are left with nothing more to do. The example of good behavior, reason, love, and kindness can accomplish a lot in securing desirable behavior (more with some children than others). Parents should instruct their children from the Word of God and depend upon the power of God's Word and His Spirit to make them like Christ. One should not be quick or eager to discipline, but we must retain that tool in our arsenal and use it when needed. There are parents who contend they love a child too much to discipline him or her. In reality such a parent loves himself too much to tolerate his own discomfort with the child's pain and resentment, and for that reason fails to do what is really needed for the child's benefit. "He who spares his rod hates his son, but he who loves him disciplines him promptly (Proverbs 13:24)."

Respect and Submission to Lawful Authority

God is the ultimate authority over His creation and over each of us. He teaches us that we are to trust Him, to gladly submit to His authority and obey Him. He has revealed in the Bible that we should not live chaotic but orderly lives, and when we do so it produces many benefits for us, for those whom we love, and for society in general. When one observes people who are in perpetual stress, crisis, and conflict, normally it is because they live chaotic lives that are not ordered according to the Word of God. They resent rules and authority (boundaries) and are quick to rebel, self-indulgent, or simply lazy.

I do not suggest one should submit to everyone who attempts to tell us what to do or that we accept all rules. It is God who establishes legitimate authority. We need to determine if the authority is legitimate, and if the rules agree with the principles of the Word of God, the Bible. When that is the case one should respectfully and gladly submit, knowing it will be for his good. When that is not the case, then one can respectfully explain why he cannot conform, but we should be very careful about doing that when we are quite young and the authority figure has much more life experience. One ought not rebel just because he is a rebel at heart nor reject traditions only because they are traditions. If we reject all traditions, we will shortly establish others that may have less to commend them to us or we will act on whim and live in chaos. In such a case, one puts himself in the category with Satan and, unless converted, will experience God's judgment.

"A brother offended is harder to win than a strong city, and contentions are like the bars of a castle (Proverbs 18:19)."

"For rebellion is as the sin of witchcraft, and stubbornness is as iniquity and idolatry (1 Samuel 15:23a)."

"Let every soul be subject to the governing authorities. For there is no authority except from God, and the authorities that exist are appointed by God. Therefore, whoever resists the authority resists the ordinance of God, and those who resist will bring judgment on themselves (Romans 13:1, 2)." "But He gives more grace. Therefore, He says: "God resists the proud, but gives grace to the humble (James 4:6)."

"Likewise, you younger people, submit yourselves to your elders. Yes, all of you be submissive to one another, and be clothed with humility, for "God resists the proud, but gives grace to the humble (1 Peter 5:5)."

Friendship, Loyalty
"A friend loves at all times, And a brother is born for adversity."—Proverbs 17:17

Everything in life, whether joy or pain, is better when we share it with someone we love, whether our spouse, parents, children, or a dear friend. Many of those who consult a psychotherapist (like me) do so simply because they do not have a friend in whom they can confide. In many churches the relationships between the members are so superficial that they could not qualify as even the most casual of friendships. Such things ought not to be and need not be. Such a congregation ought not be thought of as a Christian church.

In those moments in life when we each desperately need a faithful, dependable, compassionate friend but such a friend is lacking, it is usually because we have not bothered to be a friend and develop lasting friendships. There are many things (work, recreation, etc.) that one can allow to attract his attention to the extent that he neglects to cultivate real, lasting friendships or neglects his responsibilities to family and/or friends, but I believe if one does so, he will probably end his (or her) life with a sense of great shame, loss, and sorrow, only at the end realizing what is really important.

To be a real faithful friend is much more important than just performing religious practices. Certainly, there are things that Christians are taught to do in the way of religious practices that are good and worthwhile to do, but if one is ever faced with the necessity of choosing between a religious activity and showing love by serving a friend or family member with a pressing need, it is always preferred to do the latter.

"But the fruit of the Spirit is love, joy, peace, longsuffering, kindness, goodness, faithfulness, gentleness, self-control. Against such there is no law (Galatians 5:22, 23)."

"Greater love has no one than this, than to lay down one's life for his friends (John 15:13)."

Humility

Humility is accurately perceiving our position and value in the eyes of God and in relationship to others. It is understanding we are not inherently more important than others nor are they better than us. We all would deserve only judgment from God did He not choose to give us mercy and grace through Christ's atonement for us. Christ Jesus, the God-Man, gave us the perfect example of meekness/humility when He took the place of a servant and washed His apostles' feet. He told us to follow His example and be glad to serve rather than wanting to rule. Similarly, Moses was called the meekest man (at that time) in all the earth. He was strong in insisting on obedience to God and reverence for Him, but he would not defend himself from personal attacks.

Our contemporary culture knows nothing about humility and does not value it. Instead, it fosters pride and arrogance, things that God hates. It tells people that they can do anything they choose to do, although that is manifestly false. During one person's lifetime there will be a very small number of presidents of the United States and only a few more members of the United States Supreme Court. Anyone can aspire to one of those posts and might possibly achieve it, but it is very clear that not everyone can secure them; we will not have 350 million presidents or justices! None of us has a lack of self-esteem—perhaps self-confidence or confidence in God—but not a deficit of self-esteem. That is simply another term for self-love. God made us to care enough about ourselves so that we do the things necessary for our own well-being as we perceive it, but we are not to be our own god. Those who engage in that level of self-adulation do great harm to others and are never able to find lasting happiness. Such happiness is only found in giving God first place in our lives and learning to find pleasure in helping others.

When people talk about their rights, what they deserve, they are ignoring what the Bible says. It says there are "none righteous, there are none who understand and seek after God (Romans 3:10, 11)." That is the case when one is without the Word of God and His Spirit to illuminate our understanding and change our affections and our will (1 Corinthians 2:11–14). Without that, we will attempt to justify ourselves in everything we do while knowing full well we have had deplorable thoughts and done despicable things. According to the Bible we deserve nothing but judgment from God, every one of us, but through the life, death, and resurrection of Christ He offers us undeserved mercy, favor, and pardon. No one can receive those blessings from God without first recognizing and confessing his/her sinfulness and merit of God's judgment, and trusting in Christ and the efficacy of His work to put away our sin.

"Blessed are the meek, for they shall inherit the earth (Matthew 5:5)."

"And whoever exalts himself will be humbled, and he who humbles himself will be exalted (Matthew 23:12)."

"But He gives more grace. Therefore He says: "God resists the proud, But gives grace to the humble." Therefore submit to God. Resist the devil and he will flee from you. Draw near to God and He will draw near to you. Cleanse your hands, you sinners; and purify your hearts, you double-minded. Lament and mourn and weep! Let your laughter be turned to mourning and your joy to gloom. Humble yourselves in the sight of the Lord, and He will lift you up (James 4:6–10)."

"For thus says the High and Lofty One/Who inhabits eternity, whose Name is Holy: "I dwell in the high and holy place, with him who has a contrite and humble spirit, to revive the spirit of the humble, and to revive the heart of the contrite ones (Isaiah 57:15)." This has no reference to one's "unalienable rights" that are cited in the United States Declaration of Independence. Those are in relationship to other men, and we should claim and defend them not only for ourselves but also for the benefit of others, all the while knowing that in relationship to God we can claim no rights except those He chooses to give us when He makes us His children.

Repentance

The Bible talks quite a lot about repentance, mostly in the New Testament.

"Repent therefore and be converted, that your sins may be blotted out, so that times of refreshing may come from the presence of the Lord (Acts 3:19)."

"I tell you, no; but unless you repent you will all likewise perish (Luke 13:3)."

It does so because we have all sinned (Romans 3:23), chosen and done that which we knew to be wrong, and sadly, shamefully, we continue to do so altogether too frequently, when God through His Word admonishes us to repent. The word repent means to begin to think (and choose) differently about God, ourselves, and our behavior, and our relationship with and responsibility to other people. When we do that, it is because God has, with His Spirit, made an internal change in us.

"Then God has also granted to the Gentiles repentance to life (Acts 11:18; 16:14)."

We were previously living primarily selfish lives, going our own way. Now we have come to care more about pleasing Christ, we've begun to follow Him, and also to love and care for other people. We still stumble sometime and do what is wrong, but that is not the primary characteristic of believer's lives. We are characterized by love, righteousness, mercy, etc. (all the things I've been writing about), and when we fail, we quickly realize it, regret it, ask for pardon from Christ and any person we've wronged, we try to make amends, and resolve never to do that again, knowing that we can only succeed through the presence of the Holy Spirit and the mind of Christ that He forms within us.

An unbeliever can be content in sin; a real Christian cannot. Repentance and faith in Christ are inseparably connected to one another, as the two sides of one coin. We were trusting our own judgment and living for ourselves, and at the same time that God brought us to understand that wasn't working so well for us (we needed help), He "revealed" Christ to us as the Savior whom we need, the One who loves us, who knows what we need, the One who is all-powerful and can help us, and being all of that, the One who is worthy of our love, trust, admiration, and obedience. So, we reversed course, we were converted, changed, given a new spiritual birth, we stopped going our own way and started following Christ.

"Then He said to them all, 'If anyone desires to come after Me, let him deny himself, and take up his cross daily, and follow Me. For whoever desires to save his life will lose it, but whoever loses his life for My sake will save it" (Luke 9:23, 24). All of that happens because, and only because, God had mercy on us and granted us His grace (undeserved favor), not because we are better, smarter, wiser than anyone else. I said that the foregoing things are true of us, that they have happened to us. That is so of those who belong to Christ, and I pray it is true of you. If you are not certain, then please begin to talk to Him about it and seek Him until you have confidence based on the Word of God and His work in your life. Read **1 John** carefully. It will tell you in four specific verses how you can know that you know Christ. Immediately below are a few other verses that describe how God transforms depraved sinners and makes them His children.

"Do you not know that the unrighteous will not inherit the kingdom of God? Do not be deceived. Neither fornicators, nor idolaters, nor adulterers, nor homosexuals, nor sodomites, nor thieves, nor covetous, nor drunkards, nor revilers, nor extortioners will inherit the kingdom of God. And such were some of you. But you were washed, but you were sanctified, but you were justified in the name of the Lord Jesus and by the Spirit of our God (1 Corinthians 6:9–11)." "But God, who is rich in mercy, because of His great love with which He loved us, even when we were dead in trespasses, made us alive together with Christ (by grace you have been saved), and raised us up together, and made us sit together in the heavenly places in Christ Jesus, that in the ages to come He might show the exceeding riches of His grace in His kindness toward us in Christ Jesus. For by grace you have been saved through faith, and that not of yourselves; it is the gift of God, not of works, lest anyone should boast. For we are His workmanship, created in Christ Jesus for good works, which God prepared beforehand that we should walk in them (Ephesians 2:4–10)."

"Just as He chose us in Him before the foundation of the world, that we should be holy and without blame before Him in love (Ephesians 1:4)."

"And we know that all things work together for good to those who love God, to those who are the called according to His purpose. For whom He foreknew, He also predestined to be conformed to the image of His Son, that He might be the firstborn among many brethren. Moreover, whom He predestined, these He also called; whom He called, these He also justified; and whom He justified, these He also glorified (Romans 8:28–30)."

"For He says to Moses, "I will have mercy on whomever I will have mercy, and I will have compassion on whomever I will have compassion." So then it is not of him who wills, nor of him who runs, but of God who shows mercy (Romans 9:15).""

"And if by grace, then it is no longer of works; otherwise, grace is no longer grace. But if it is of works, it is no longer grace; otherwise, work is no longer work (Romans 11:6).""

Pardon, Forgiveness

When we ask for pardon, whether of God or man, we are acknowledging that we have committed an offense, and we ask that the guilt of that offense be canceled out, not charged against us, and that we thus be not punished for the offense. "Blessed is he whose transgression is forgiven, whose sin is covered. Blessed is the man to whom the LORD does not impute iniquity, and in whose spirit there is no deceit (Psalm 32:1, 2)."

There is a significant difference between saying only "I am sorry," or saying "excuse me," and saying, "I am sorry, please pardon me." (Never say, "I apologize"—that is form without content.) When I ask for pardon, I acknowledge that I am guilty of an offense and deserving of a penalty; it implies that I wish I could undo the matter and do it again differently; it acknowledges that the offended party would be justified in requiring some payment of me for my offense (or excluding me from his friendship); and it asks that the person offended grant the kindness that only nobility can, that is, simply to cancel out my offense, while acknowledging he has the power to pardon me or demand restitution.

God will pardon us when He has brought us to repentance and faith in Christ. There are times when we need others to pardon us also, and we need to do the same for others. It can only happen when the offense is treated as a serious matter, and the pardon as a great and precious gift not to be taken for granted nor abused. We have offended God and we need pardon. We wrong others and need their pardon. Others wrong us and need our pardon. The willingness to confess our wrongdoing, repent and seek pardon, and to pardon others when they show repentance and seek pardon, is critical to success in relationships with God, our spouse, and with others.

"For if you forgive men their trespasses, your heavenly Father will also forgive you: But if you do not forgive men their trespasses, neither will your Father forgive your trespasses (Matthew 6:14, 15)." Please note this is God's Word and will always be accomplished!

"Judge not, and you shall not be judged. Condemn not, and you shall not be condemned. Forgive, and you will be forgiven (Luke 6:37)."

"For judgment is without mercy to the one who has shown no mercy. Mercy triumphs over judgment (James 2:13)."

"Yes, and why, even of yourselves, do you not judge what is right (Luke 12:57)?"

"Do not judge according to appearance, but judge with righteous judgment (John 7:24)."

Assurance of Salvation but Not Presumption

This involves two questions that are related but not the same: "How can I be saved?" And then, "How can I know I am saved?" There are people who think they are saved but are not because they are trusting in something other than Christ (parents' religion, baptism, church membership, good works, etc.). There are others who are saved but who for various reasons (anxiety over past sins, etc.) lack confidence and peace.

First, one should understand the Bible teaches (in Scripture we have cited above) that one is saved (forgiven, has peace with God and eternal life) only through trusting in Christ—trusting that the Son of God was born as the infant Jesus, became a man and fulfilled for us all the righteousness of the law of God, died for our sins on the cross, was buried and then arose defeating sin and death, and ascended to the right hand of the Father where He lives and forever makes intercession for His people. We receive the benefit of Christ's life and work only because God grants us favor to trust Him, trust He is who He said He was, trust He did and will do what He said He would do, trust every word He has given us in the Bible is true, and trust that His will and way for us in every moment is the best of all possible options. Such trust will cause us to follow and obey His Word.

Presuming on the grace of God would be to presume that because we have gone through the motions and appear to have done what people told us we must do to be saved, that we are then saved even if/when there is no evidence of God's transforming grace in our lives, no love for God or others, and no interest in obeying the Word of God and actually following Christ. So how can one have a good basis for confidence that his religion is not just a pretense and that he has actually been converted and can be at peace knowing that Christ will keep forever those whom He has chosen and converted?

The apostle John answers that in 1 John. He says, "These things I have written to you who believe in the name of the Son of God, that you may know that you have eternal life, and that you may continue to believe in the name of the Son of God. (1 John 5:13)" One should not underestimate the importance of this statement: Christ grants repentance and faith to those He has chosen, and then He saves us when we trust in Him (Acts 16:31, Romans 4:24, Romans 10:13; Ephesians 1:13). **But how do I know that I have the kind or level of trust in Christ of which the Scripture speaks?** John gives us three proofs that we have saving faith. Proof number one is, Christians habitually obey God's commands. First, John says, "Now by this we know that we know Him, if we keep His commandments. He who says, 'I know Him,' and does not keep His commandments, is a liar, and the truth is not in him (1 John 2:3, 4)." John, writing under the inspiration of the Holy Spirit, is not saying that we always keep the Word of God perfectly and never sin. There is plenty of evidence in the scriptures that no on does or can do that, and we often sorrow over our failure, seeking forgiveness and grace to do better. As long as believers are living on earth, they are in the process of being perfected, being made like Christ. But we love God and our neighbors; we love righteousness and want to do what is right and pleasing to God.

Our usual practice is to obey God, to keep His commandments. That is not the usual practice of those who do not trust in Christ. They are enemies of Christ. We are not. We are sorry and ashamed when we fail Him. If one has no interest in being with the people of God and obeying Him, then such a person has no biblical basis for believing he or she has peace with God and eternal life. Christians are not yet perfected, so they are vulnerable to temptation, faulty judgment, and sin. But they do have the life of Christ within them, so they trust Him, and obedience to Him is an essential and preponderant characteristic of their lives. If it is not, then such a person has not really been born again by God's Spirit (John 3:5-8; 1 Peter 1:3–23).

Another basis John gives us for confidence in our relationship with Christ is found in 1 John 3:14. There he says, "We know that we have passed from death to life, because we love the brethren. He who does not love his brother abides in death." He is speaking here of our brethren in Christ, but that surely applies to those of our own family, and Christ also commanded us to love our neighbors and even our enemies. Paul says in Romans 5:5, "-the love of God has been poured out into our hearts by the Holy Spirit." If our life is not characterized by love then we do not have the Spirit of God within us and are not of God (Romans 8:9). This love is not just an emotion but causes us to seek the well-being of another ahead of our own interests. It will cause us to restrain our tongue, to defer to another, to avoid engaging in conflict, and to forgive. Do you love the people of God and enjoy being with them?

The third evidence John gives us that we have been born again of God and have His life within us is in 1 John 4:13. Here he says, "By this we know that we abide in Him, and He in us, because He has given us of His Spirit." God's Spirit within us gives us the sense that He is our Father and we are His children. Paul says in Romans 8:15, 16, "-you received the Spirit of adoption by whom we cry out, 'Abba, Father.' The Spirit Himself bears witness with our spirit that we are children of God." So there are three evidences that serve as a strong basis for confidence that we are not deluded and trusting in our own works or in religious traditions but that we really belong to Christ: 1) We practice obeying Christ as He speaks to us in His Word; 2) We are loving people and we show that love by our word and our behavior; and finally, 3) God's Spirit lives within us and gives us

103

a sense that we belong to Him, that God is our Father and we are His children (Romans 8:15; Galatians 4:6).

Patience, Perseverance

The apostle Paul teaches us in Galatians 5 that the Holy Spirit produces certain qualities in those in whom He lives; they are called the "fruit of the Spirit," and one of them is longsuffering or patience. Patience is the trait of remaining relatively calm in difficult circumstances and, while doing what we can to resolve the matter, not despairing but waiting for God to help us or arrange the matter according to His own plan and in His time. It may be when one is suffering with bad health and the matter may not involve anyone else and their behavior, or it may be when another person is behaving inappropriately and causing us real difficulty. We may handle it without distress because of our knowledge that God is in control and because He commands us to love our enemies and will enable us to have compassion on those who lack the fruit of the Spirit because the Holy Spirit does not live within them. But we are unlikely to have that charitable attitude unless we have studied God's Word and have its perspective within us.

It may also help us if we remember there have probably been occasions when our behavior was a provocation to others and we needed their patience and not a very severe reproof or discipline. Most people fail in that respect. They are easily angered and quick to vent their anger to those who do not please them. They are unaware when they are displaying a lack of spiritual maturity, kindness, and self- control. Such a person can be manipulated by another simply by provoking their anger. Know that patience is a virtue; make it one of your goals to be a patient person, to control your tongue, and weigh your words before speaking.

"Even a fool is counted wise when he holds his peace: when he shuts his lips he is considered perceptive (Proverbs 17:28, KJV)."

"Love suffers long and is kind; love does not envy; love does not parade itself, is not puffed up; does not behave rudely, does not seek its own, is not provoked, thinks no evil (1 Cor. 13:4, 5)."

"But he who endures to the end shall be saved (Matthew 24:13)." "Therefore, as the elect of God, holy and beloved, put on tender mercies, kindness, humility, meekness, longsuffering; bearing with one another, and forgiving one another, if anyone has a complaint against another; even as Christ forgave you, so you also must do (Colossians 3:12, 13)."

"The LORD is merciful and gracious, slow to anger, and abounding in mercy (Psalm 103:8)."

Courage and Endurance

"Be strong and of good courage, do not fear nor be afraid of them; for the LORD your God, He is the One who goes with you. He will not leave you nor forsake you (Deuteronomy 31:6)."

There are twenty-two verses in the King James version of the Bible that admonish us to possess courage. Most of those are in the Old Testament, but many in the New Testament tell us we are in a spiritual warfare and we must be strong, resist evil, and resist the devil (James 4:7; 1 Peter 5:9; 1 Corinthians 16:13; Ephesians 6:10–18). A conservative author whom I appreciate avows that courage is the most important of character attributes. That is because on many occasions it will be costly, even dangerous, to consistently embrace and uphold the values of truth, morality, love, and righteousness that the Word of God expounds, the Church has upheld for two thousand years, and we espouse in this book. The values we have discussed above are among the communicable attributes of God, which is to say those He shares with us and that through His grace we humans who are His followers may also come to possess. (His incommunicable attributes, like omnipotence, omniscience, omnipresence, are His exclusively; no one else can possess them.)

The Bible is very clear that there is an evil personality, called the devil or Satan, who has been adamantly opposed to God since prior to the creation of man. He was originally created by God, but it seems that he rebelled and fell from the high estate that he once held. He is not equal to God and cannot effectively oppose God directly, so in his hostility he attacks mankind whom God originally created similar to Himself. If you embrace these values of godliness that we are discussing it will be because God has chosen you (John 15:16; Ephesians 1:4, 5; Romans 8:28–32), given you a new spiritual birth to eternal life (John 3), and drawn you to Himself (John 6:37, 44), making you His child. Because of that the diabolical enemy of God, and those whom he has deceived and who follow him (many unwittingly), will attack you, tempt you, and try to deceive you and/or destroy you. That battle will continue unrelenting all your life.

Our Lord told us clearly in Luke 14:27–33 that when we consider following Him, we must count the cost, be prepared, and take our cross daily and follow Him. He said without that we cannot be His disciple/follower, a Christian. All of this seems to have been widely understood in our country for perhaps one hundred fifty years as well as that there is a tension between the Lord's Church (those who belong to Him) and the world system that belongs to the wicked one.

Biblical values of honesty and morality were once admired in our culture such that, at the time of my conversion to follow Christ in 1963, I believed a person could not be successful in life without a Christian testimony. That is no longer the majority belief in our culture. Profanity is common in public discourse, and we no longer expect public figures to possess admirable character. The examples of those who maintain moral integrity serve as a reproof to the perverse and corrupt and cause the righteous (not self-righteous) to be despised and attacked. An excellent example is the ridicule Vice-President Mike Pence incurred when he revealed his practice of never meeting alone with a woman other than his wife.

Men, Women, Marriage, Sex, and Love

Some people would not believe this topic is appropriate to be included in the present volume; that it is too "earthy," not spiritual enough. I disagree and have decided to include it because we are discussing how to have a a good life, and the inability of a husband and wife to develop and maintain a mutually satisfying sexual relationship is one of the three primary causes of marital unhappiness and failure.

During the last 37 years I have occasionally received a certain kind of letter from an unhappy wife. Actually, it is usually my wife who receives it and shares it with me, because at this point these women have decided that all men are beasts and they have no interest in confiding in any man. The letter is usually from a young wife and goes like this: "My husband is a beast; all he ever thinks about is sex." From there, the details vary but are examples to illustrate this persuasion: my husband (and all men) are beasts, and think only about sex. I will respond first to the women who find themselves in this dilemma and reach this conclusion, and then to their husbands, for both have responsibility in the matter. I will offer occasional observations to the both, because although the biblical roles are different for husband and wife, as is the genetic equipment God gave them for these roles, there are many biblical precepts and principles that are equally applicable to all.

My response to this wife is, No, it is highly unlikely that your husband is a beast, and that he thinks only about sex. He is a man, in such a case usually a young one, who is alive, hopefully reasonably healthy, and with a strong charge of testosterone coursing through his body. He does not think only about sex, but he does think about sex a great deal. He thinks about sex when he awakes in the morning, when he is eating as well as before and after he eats, when he is driving, when he is working, when he is playing, when he is resting, before he goes to sleep, etc. You fill in the blank. The evidence is clear that he does many other things besides think of sex, so he must think of these other things also. He just thinks about sex while he is doing the other things, before, after, and probably more than any of them. He is also probably young, inexperienced, impulsive, and selfish. He may be driven, controlled by his impulses rather than his knowledge of the Word and will of God and his love for others, especially his wife; although he very well may think that his sexual desire for his wife is love. His sexual behavior should be an expression of his love for his wife; but if so, it will be disciplined, moderated by his desire to seek her satisfaction and well-being.

The real problem is that this wife and her husband have not learned to talk to and listen to one another, understand, love (delight in giving priority to the needs and interests), and show love for one another; and there is no functional difference in these latter two. Love that isn't demonstrated doesn't count; it is worthless (Prov.27:5). What is commonly believed to be love for another is very often nothing but self-love. It is the warm pleasant feeling (romance) one enjoys when with another special person; another who is attractive, well-attired, who smells good, is thoughtful, a pleasant conversationalist, etc. The critical element here is that subjective enjoyment is the essential ingredient, and that is certainly not so with Christian love. (read I Cor. 13) In romance there is no lasting commitment to the well-being of the other or to perform ones word, to keep the promises that were made to live exclusively with one another and serve one another "as long as you both shall live." When the warm little glow is no longer present, when one is no longer the center of attention, when the other person is annoying, demanding, unattractive (for whatever reasons), when one must deal with the responsibilities of marriage and a family, and when the experience is no longer pleasant and convenient, far too many people very rapidly fall out of romance (not love!).

The way God made men, they do not require a great deal of external stimulation to cause them sexual excitement. Often just elapsed time and body chemistry is enough, without any external provocation. But the sight of an interesting curve, a bit of bare skin, or the anticipation of intimate interaction with his wife can in a moment get a man highly charged and ready for action. That is the way men are. That is the way God made them; but they still need to learn to discipline their thinking and impulses to honor God and their wives. Although a young wife may not have understood it, this is the kind of person to whom she was attracted, and to whom she vowed a life-long commitment. What is the value of your word, and especially when you invoke God as witness? Do you speak the truth and perform your commitments whether convenient or not?

None of this means the husband is blameless, that he isn't selfish, that he understands his wife as he should, and is as considerate of her wants and needs as he should be. His turn comes next, and that will be his problem. The wife's problem is primarily herself, and whether she is a knowledgeable, and understanding woman of integrity who has the capacity to love another and persist in a faithful commitment to seek the well-being and happiness of her husband and do so "as unto the Lord." Look at John 21:22 and we see that Christ's charge to each of us is unconditional, without regard to whether another, even the spouse does as he or she should. Another's poor conduct is never an adequate excuse that will cause the Lord to ignore disobedient, selfish, petulant behavior.

The idea, the purpose, of the marriage relationship is for a man and a woman to be and do for one another what neither can do for himself or herself; to be a faithful friend/companion/supporter in serving God together; in helping one another to grow more like Christ. One cannot do that and require that he or she is constantly the center of attention; that in everything we do, it is all about me and what I want or need. When we learn to give ourselves to Christ by giving ourselves to the well-being and happiness of our spouse, we find our own happiness in doing so, even though the spouse is still far from perfect, as are we.

Most women do not respond so readily as men either to internal stimuli or to external visual stimuli. They do not think about sex all the time. They usually require vocal expressions of affection, and/or embraces and caresses from the specific man for whom they already have warm tender feelings, and either or both of these for a duration or five to fifteen minutes or longer before they experience significant sexual arousal. The men are commonly so easily and highly aroused that they enter the sexual relationship focused primarily on their own sexual fulfillment, and with little understanding or thought of what works well for their wife, and what she needs. As a result of this, a man may rush through the physical interaction of sexual relationships and be personally satisfied before his wife has hardly begun to be aroused. If that happens, unless she is an unusually mature woman this will leave her frustrated. There are some of these things that men could learn from reading appropriate clinical literature, but part of it can be learned only from experience, and a young couple should certainly not normally be well experienced in sexual relationships. That only leaves one option; they must take time, be tender and patient with one another, and learn together. The young husband and wife ought not have high expectations and demands of one another in regard to sexual matters but should be delighted that they have each honored God and one another by waiting until marriage to learn together.

When that hasn't happened and one or both have been sexually active before marriage, they should be honest and confess this to their fiancée before marriage. One cannot build a sound marriage on a foundation of lies and deceit. If they are not able to repent and forgive as required, become convinced that God has changed the offender(s), and put those sordid events behind them, they should not marry. If they do not follow that course, their profligate behavior may dog them all their years together.

In the process of getting to know one another in an intimate way each will make some mistakes and time will be required. They must both be patient, be gentle and thoughtful of the needs and desires of the other, and it is highly important that they talk openly and specifically to one another about what works and doesn't work for them in the sexual relationship. Both should be open and assertive in suggesting and discouraging techniques, frequency, etc. Anything is OK that is not compulsive, that is not painful or harmful in some way, that respects the volition and the dignity of both parties, that is pleasurable and satisfying, and that is not directly contrary to scripture. When one does not know what "works" for him or her, he or she has the responsibility to ask their spouse's help, experimenting together, until they find out. When they do not do so, and learn how to enjoy the sexual relationship, then it is not likely that either will long have the level of enjoyment and satisfaction that they could and should. In such a case at least one or the other will be unhappy, and because of his or her behavior the other will be unhappy, and both will be vulnerable to suggestions and temptations of Satan in this matter.

I Peter 3:7 says, "Husbands, likewise, dwell with them [your wife] with understanding, giving honor to the wife, as to the weaker vessel, and as being heirs together of the grace of life, that your prayers may not be hindered." This passage means a husband does not need to "understand women," but he needs to seriously apply himself to understand this one woman, and it applies equally to the woman's responsibility to understand her husband and seek his happiness. That will require patience, asking questions, listening, etc. But one cannot know another who does not wish to be known, so she/he must take the responsibility for self-disclosure; for telling the spouse what is wanted and needed. This requires a certain vulnerability and humility.

It is not selfish to ask for what one wants and/or needs as long as it is not without consideration of the other. It is an acknowledgement of dependency; that I am not sufficient alone and I need this person to do for me what I cannot do for myself. One reason people find it so difficult is because of their pride, or to say it differently: fear of rejection and humiliation. To ask is to express confidence in the love of one's spouse and to invest in the happiness of both. To not ask for what one needs and wants in this relationship amounts to a lack of confidence that God is working for good in every event in the lives of those who belong to Him (Romans 8:28). "Perfect love casts our fear (I Jn. 4:18)". If you are a believer, God has brought this person, your husband or wife, with all his or her strengths and faults into your life, so that you can complement one another in the process of growing to become like Christ (Rom. 8:29).

There is no place for demands in this relationship. The husband and wife should each give the other constant ample reassurance for knowing that his or her spouse wants to give the other things and do things that he or she will enjoy; so that each will not be afraid to express their desires. Then, because this, like most of our relationships, is a voluntary relationship, he/she should wait and respect the right of the other to choose how and when to respond. If there are negative consequences for non-compliance, then this was not a request but a demand, and an attempt to control and exploit the other.

In I Corinthians 7:2-5 Paul shows us how the husband and wife are each to give preference to the needs and desires of the other in this matter of sexual relationships, and also that our faithfulness in doing so, or lack of it, may make us less or more vulnerable to

Satan's attacks on us through our sexual appetites. Beginning in verse two Paul says, "Nevertheless, because of sexual immorality, let each man have his own wife, and let each woman have her own husband. 3 Let the husband render to his wife the affection due her, and likewise also the wife to her husband. 4 The wife does not have authority over her own body, but the husband does. And likewise, the husband does not have authority over his own body, but the wife does. 5 Do not deprive one another except with consent for a time, that you may give yourselves to fasting and prayer; and come together again so that Satan does not tempt you because of your lack of self-control."

It is important to note several things about Paul's statement here that neither husband or wife has control of his or her own body. This certainly does not mean that each should just follow his/her own passions and impulses and do whatever and whenever with the other without regard to how it will work for the spouse. That would amount to selfish mutual exploitation, not love, it would produce an adversarial relationship, and there would be no real happiness for either in such an arrangement. That having been said, Paul is teaching that in the marriage relationship each one is accepting his/her responsibility to be available to the spouse and provide him/her sexual pleasure and satisfaction.

Loving husbands and wives should recognize this is a charge we have received from God, and we should delight in being able to do so. It is also important to note that sexual needs are not the only ones that are to be met in the marriage relationship, and others are equally legitimate. If one or the other is ill, or has physical conditions that make sexual intercourse especially difficult at a given time, the spouse should want to delay his or her own sexual impulses to care for the needs of the other. The idea is to achieve a balance by minimizing discomfort and maximizing satisfaction equally for both husband and wife.

In I Cor. 7:9 Paul is speaking of the advisability of marriage for a given person and says, "But if they cannot contain, let them marry: for it is better to marry than to burn." Some would interpret that to mean burn in the fires of hell for having lived an immoral life in rebellion against God. Many students of scripture think that it rather means having the constant inner struggle and temptation of raging sexual passions that come in part from the absence of the release, and the positive satisfaction, that God provided we should have in the marriage relationship. In either case verse five and nine both clearly show us God provided for sexual fulfillment in marriage to help us avoid being vulnerable to Satan's attacks on us through the sexual appetites. We have that resource only when husband and wife see the sexual relationship not as a thing to be despised but as a way to express love and to serve one another. If we do not work to achieve high levels of sexual satisfaction in the marriage, then we are responsible for making ourselves and our spouse vulnerable to Satan's attack in this area.

No discussion of marriage relationships is complete without considering Eph. 5:22-32, and I Cor. 13. Ephesians 5:22 commands, "Wives, submit to your own husbands, as to the Lord. 23 For the husband is head of the wife, as also Christ is head of the church; and He is the Savior of the body. 24 Therefore, just as the church is subject to Christ, so let the wives be to their own husbands in everything." Just as God gave different disciplines for Adam and Eve that were suited to their individual role and disobedience in the fall into sin, so he gives different commands to husband and wife in the marriage relationship that are suited to the characteristics He created in them, and the roles He has planned they take, complementing one another in marriage. Generally, He equips women for the nurturing mother role with an instinctive compulsion to express warm, tender affection; something that is absolutely essential for the healthy development of children. Consequently, the average woman has less need than men to be commanded to discipline herself to give constant attention to develop and achieve the capacity and practice of expressing affection.

The one thing that is critical she give attention to is respecting, trusting, and submitting to God's direction for her life as it is expressed through her husband. There are two reasons this is so important. One is that because of our rebellious sinful nature every man and every woman has a problem with authority. We inherited a rebellious nature from our first parents, and we have individually and personally rebelled against God. We must learn that is not good in any sense; that God is worthy of our love and service, and that our highest good is found in loving and serving Him. That change of mind, affections, and will, is repentance, and it must be the first and constant practice of the believer in Christ. It is very easy to profess it in relationship to God but the test of its reality is seen in how we relate to the tangible people God brings into our lives. Do we, or do we not, willingly submit to legitimate authority without resentment and resistance?

God deals with the necessity for this repentant submission in men, too. He just does it through relationships He has ordained they should have with other Christian brethren, in work relationships, and civil government. That is because one cannot lead and follow at the same time, in the same relationship. The other reason that submission is so important in the wife, is that her husband's number one responsibility, after serving and obeying God, and as assigned to him by God, is caring for his wife, with all that means. He cannot possibly succeed in this task, and maintain the confidence necessary to do so, except as she cooperates by respecting, trusting, and following him.

Husbands are commanded in Eph. 5:25-31 "Husbands, love your wives, just as Christ also loved the church and gave Himself for her, that He might sanctify and cleanse her with the washing of water by the word, that He might present her to Himself a glorious church, not having spot or wrinkle or any such thing, but that she should be holy and without blemish. So husbands ought to love their own wives as their own bodies; he who loves his wife loves himself. For no one ever hated his own flesh, but nourishes and cherishes it, just as the Lord does the church. For we are members of His body, of His flesh and of His bones. For this reason a man shall leave his father and mother and be joined to his wife, and the two shall become one flesh."

In this passage Paul addresses the unique responsibility for which God designed men, and with which He charges a man as first a husband, and then a father, and also with the weaknesses that seem to be an inevitable corollary of the strengths necessary to his role. His responsibility is to maintain a single-minded focus on obeying God in this enormously important task of caring for and protecting his wife and family, leading them in spiritual disciplines, and in a life of loving service to God and man. He must stand between his wife and children, and the deceits and assaults of this corrupt fallen world, and protect these whom God has committed to his charge. A man cannot be carried first one way and then another by his emotions and impulses and accomplish this task. He must make wise, reasoned decisions in obedience to the Word of God, and then carry through with them, even when many people may misunderstand and disagree, when he feels alone, and when all this is emotionally very painful for him.

God equips a man for this task, but the very strengths that enable him to accomplish this primary mission make it more difficult for him to engage in self-disclosure, to be vulnerable, to deal with emotions, and to express love, so that his wife feels secure in trusting him, and submitting to and following his leadership.

He may not realize that his wife is not reading his task-driven behavior as an expression of love; that he needs to carefully give her his attention, ask for her counsel, listen to her, daily tell her of his love for her, and explain how his love for God, and for his wife, is the motivating force behind each of his decisions and actions. Just as the woman must work to combat her propensity to undermine her husband's leadership by her independence, so the man must work to learn what it means to love his wife, and then consistently and carefully express that love to her. If he does not do so, she will find it very difficult to follow one whom she is not certain is always seeking her well-being.

It is also important that the husband demonstrate to his wife his submission to God through his submission to the collective judgment of Christian brethren with whom he is in relationship. This evidence of a teachable and obedient heart, consistent Christian character and behavior, and his regularly expressed love are important to show his wife that these pious religious phrases are not simply a tool to control and exploit her for his own ends. The husband and wife need frequently to read I Cor. 13 together and separately and reflect on it to be reminded that Christ's agape love that we are to have for one another is a sacrificial love that places the well-being of the beloved before one's own comfort, preference, or well-being. Christ gave His life for His Bride. That is how we are to love one another. Eph. 5:32-33 says, "This is a great mystery, but I speak concerning Christ and the church. Nevertheless, let each one of you in particular so love his own wife as himself, and let the wife see that she respects her husband."

The marriage sexual relationship can be, and should be, a source of great pleasure and joy, for both husband and wife. But to consistently achieve this potential in their moments of physical intimacy, the sexual relationship must be accepted as a means for the husband and wife to express Christ's love to one another. That love and unity they desire to experience through this special union must be expressed not only in moments of intense passion, but both before and after it must be cherished and expressed daily, all day long, in a multitude of loving words and actions.

Since I began this writing homosexual "marriage" has come to be widely accepted in our country. Many are contending that a person can be male or female, as they choose, no matter the sex with which they were born. Those who disagree are roundly castigated and, in some places, may suffer severe penalties, lose their employment, and/or be charged with a crime. That is the hostility of the forces of darkness against truth and righteousness. Our Lord was determined to go to Jerusalem in spite of knowing the indignities and suffering that awaited Him there. He had previously commanded His followers to take up the cross and follow Him, but only John and a few women stayed with Him through the crucifixion. There was much they did not understand prior to His resurrection and the coming of the Holy Spirit on the day of Pentecost to indwell and impower his Church. Since then, many believers who followed Christ have been persecuted and have borne witness with their blood of His truth and His love. We are called to be part of that company, to be faithful and endure, not knowing what persecution we may suffer (Hebrews 11).

"Have I not commanded you? Be strong and of good courage; do not be afraid, nor be dismayed, for the LORD your God is with you wherever you go (Joshua 1:9)."

"Finally, my brethren, be strong in the Lord and in the power of His might. Put on the whole armor of God, that you may be able to stand against the wiles of the devil. For we do not wrestle against flesh and blood, but against principalities, against powers, against the rulers of the darkness of this age, against spiritual hosts of wickedness in the heavenly places. Therefore, take up the whole armor of God, that you may be able to withstand in the evil day, and having done all, to stand.

Stand therefore, having girded your waist with truth, having put on the breastplate of righteousness, and having shod your feet with the preparation of the gospel of peace; above all, taking the shield of faith with which you will be able to quench all the fiery darts of the wicked one. And take the helmet of salvation, and the sword of the Spirit, which is the Word of God; praying always with all prayer and supplication in the Spirit, being watchful to this end with all perseverance and supplication for all the saints (Ephesians 6:10–18)."

"And because lawlessness will abound, the love of many will grow cold. But he who endures to the end shall be saved (Matthew 24:12, 13)."

****

It is likely that I have overlooked something really important, and I trust that some of you will remind me and give me reason to begin another labor of love.

Please know and remember that the above principles of ethical and moral Christian behavior are just as applicable in the marriage relationship and in the parent-child relationship as they are in all others. I will look to see you in eternity with our Lord, and our Mamaw (Caraleen), Mrs. Charlene, and all our family together. Be sure you do not fail of the grace of God so you will be there with us (Hebrews 12:15).

With very much love always! Papaw

Citizenship Imposes Obligations on a Christian

Blessed is the nation whose God is the LORD, the people He has chosen as His own inheritance.

Psalm 33:12

We, in the democratic Republic of the United States of America, have been given a government of the People, by the People, and for the People, and with it the recognition of the right to "Life, Liberty, and the Pursuit of Happiness." I am very thankful to our God and Father for the pleasant conditions and the opportunities our government and society has provided us, but I will not argue that all of the details of our government and society are clearly set forth in Scripture. They are not. Some but not all of the founders of our nation were Christian, but I know of none who dissented from the view that mankind was created by an omnipotent, just, and kind Creator who bestowed on us the right to life, liberty, and the pursuit of happiness. It seems that many if not all the Founders believed that the kind of democratic republic, they bequeathed to us was "wholly inadequate to any but a moral and religious people (John Adams)."

There has always been crime and immorality among us as there is in every society of sinful men, and we were slow to rectify some of the abominable practices among us (e.g., slavery), but we did so because of the influence of the gospel among us, and far earlier than many other nations. Since the dawn of civilization, slavery had been common in almost every human society and still today continues in some, but the principles that provided for the eradication of slavery were included in our Declaration of Independence and our Constitution although not then explicitly applied to the issue. The Church pressed for the abolition of slavery until it was achieved first in England and then in the United States of America. In the United States, the Church has advanced the greatest Christian missionary movement in history and demonstrated Christ's love by building and operating hospitals and orphanages.

Now in the twenty-first century, there are socio-political forces openly working in the United States and exerting great influence to pervert and eradicate our true history and values, to deny to our citizens the "unalienable rights" granted to us by God and clearly acknowledged in our founding documents, and to bring us under a tyrannical totalitarian government that is hostile to Christianity. Our nation is unique in the history of the world. I know of no other nation who has approximated the level of peace, prosperity, and justice that we have enjoyed, except perhaps Israel when for brief periods she was under the direction of some of her judges, and perhaps a very few righteous kings.

Every American should familiarize himself with our constitutional rights and obligations, be very grateful for the unique blessings we have received from God, and work to preserve them. For that purpose, I am appending immediately below the text of the Declaration of Independence proclaimed by the founders of our nation, and, following it, the Constitution of the United States of America. All who believe in one sovereign, omnipotent, and righteous Creator God will understand that He appointed us to this time and place in history and the blessings they bring us, be grateful, and work to defend and maintain this tranquil and prosperous state.

"Render to Caesar the things that are Caesar's, and to God the things that are God's (Mark 12:17)."

"Let every soul be subject to the governing authorities. For there is no authority except from God, and the authorities that exist are appointed by God (Romans 13:1)."

I pray you will read and love these proclamations, commit to memory many of the principles and actively work to preserve the representative republic that they describe. You may do so by passing on the understanding of our heritage to your children as well as by exercising your First Amendment rights, participating in the political process, and, if need be, taking up arms to defend the fundamental essence of the nation for which the founders pledged their "lives, fortunes, and sacred honour."

The Declaration of Independence of the United States of America

IN CONGRESS, JULY 4, 1776
The unanimous Declaration of the thirteen United States of America,

WHEN in the Course of human Events, it becomes necessary for one People to dissolve the Political Bands which have connected them with another, and to assume among the Powers of the Earth, the separate and equal Station to which the Laws of Nature and of Nature's God entitle them, a decent Respect to the Opinions of Mankind requires that they should declare the causes which impel them to the Separation.

We hold these Truths to be self-evident, that all Men are created equal, that they are endowed by their Creator with certain unalienable Rights, that among these are Life, Liberty and the pursuit of Happiness. —That to secure these Rights, Governments are instituted among Men, deriving their just Powers from the Consent of the Governed, —That whenever any Form of Government becomes destructive of these Ends, it is the Right of the People to alter or to abolish it, and to institute new Government, laying its Foundation on such Principles and organizing its Powers in such Form, as to them shall seem most likely to effect their Safety and Happiness. Prudence, indeed, will dictate that Governments long established should not be changed for light and transient

Causes; and accordingly all Experience hath shewn, that Mankind are more disposed to suffer, while Evils are sufferable, than to right themselves by abolishing the Forms to which they are accustomed. But when a long Train of Abuses and Usurpations, pursuing invariably the same Object evinces a Design to reduce them under absolute Despotism, it is their Right, it is their Duty, to throw off such Government, and to provide new Guards for their future Security. Such has been the patient Sufferance of these Colonies; and such is now the Necessity which constrains them to alter their former Systems of Government. The History of the present King of Great Britain is a History of repeated injuries and Usurpations, all having in direct Object the Establishment of an absolute Tyranny over these States. To prove this, let Facts be submitted to a candid World.

He has refused his Assent to Laws, the most wholesome and necessary for the public Good.

He has forbidden his Governors to pass Laws of immediate and pressing Importance, unless suspended in their Operation till his Assent should be obtained; and when so suspended, he has utterly neglected to attend to them.

He has refused to pass other Laws for the Accommodation of large Districts of People, unless those People would relinquish the Right of Representation in the Legislature, a Right inestimable to them, and formidable to Tyrants only.

He has called together Legislative Bodies at Places unusual, uncomfortable, and distant from the Depository of their public Records, for the sole Purpose of fatiguing them into Compliance with his Measures.

He has dissolved Representative Houses repeatedly, for opposing with manly Firmness his Invasions on the Rights of the People.

He has refused for a long Time, after such Dissolutions, to cause others to be elected; whereby the Legislative Powers, incapable of Annihilation, have returned to the People at large for their exercise; the State remaining in the mean-time exposed to all the Dangers of Invasion from without, and Convulsions within.

He has endeavoured to prevent the Population of these States; for that Purpose obstructing the Laws for Naturalization of Foreigners; refusing to pass others to encourage their Migrations hither, and raising the Conditions of new Appropriations of Lands.

He has obstructed the Administration of Justice, by ref He has made Judges dependent on his Will alone, for the Tenure of their Offices, and the Amount and Payment of their Salaries.

He has erected a Multitude of New Offices, and sent hither Swarms of Officers to harass our People, and eat out their Substance.

He has kept among us, in Times of Peace, Standing Armies without the Consent of our Legislatures.

He has affected to render the Military independent of and superior to the Civil Power.

He has combined with others to subject us to a Jurisdiction foreign to our Constitution, and unacknowledged by our Laws; giving his Assent to their Acts of pretended Legislation:

For quartering large Bodies of Armed Troops among us:

For protecting them, by a mock Trial, from Punishment for any Murders which they should commit on the Inhabitants of these States:

For cutting off our Trade with all Parts of the World:

For imposing Taxes on us without our Consent:

For depriving us, in many Cases, of the Benefits of Trial by Jury:

For transporting us beyond Seas to be tried for pretended Offences: For abolishing the free System of English Laws in a neighbouring Province, establishing therein an arbitrary Government, and enlarging its Boundaries, so as to render it at once an Example and fit Instrument for introducing the same absolute Rule into these Colonies:

For taking away our Charters, abolishing our most valuable Laws, and altering fundamentally the Forms of our Governments:

For suspending our own Legislatures, and declaring themselves invested with Power to legislate for us in all

Cases whatsoever. He has abdicated Government here, by declaring us out of his Protection and waging War against us.

He has plundered our Seas, ravaged our Coasts, burnt our Towns, and destroyed the Lives of our People.

He is, at this Time, transporting large Armies of foreign Mercenaries to compleat the Works of Death, Desolation, and Tyranny, already begun with circumstances of Cruelty & Perfidy, scarcely paralleled in the most barbarous Ages, and totally unworthy the Head of a civilized Nation.

He has constrained our fellow Citizens taken Captive on the high Seas to bear Arms against their Country, to become the Executioners of their Friends and Brethren, or to fall themselves by their Hands.

He has excited domestic Insurrections amongst us, and has endeavoured to bring on the Inhabitants of our frontiers, the merciless Indian Savages, whose known Rule of Warfare, is an undistinguished Destruction of all Ages, Sexes and Conditions.

In every stage of these Oppressions we have Petitioned for Redress in the most humble Terms: Our repeated Petitions have been answered only by repeated Injury. A Prince whose Character is thus marked by every act which may define a Tyrant, is unfit to be the Ruler of a free People.

Nor have we been wanting in Attentions to our British Brethren. We have warned them from Time to Time of

133

Attempts by their Legislature to extend an unwarrantable Jurisdiction over us. We have reminded them of the Circumstances of our Emigration and Settlement here. We have appealed to their native Justice and Magnanimity, and we have conjured them by the Ties of our common Kindred to disavow these Usurpations, which, would inevitably interrupt our Connections and Correspondence. They too have been deaf to the Voice of Justice and of Consanguinity. We must, therefore, acquiesce in the Necessity, which denounces our Separation, and hold them, as we hold the rest of Mankind, Enemies in War, in Peace, Friends.

We, therefore, the Representatives of the UNITED STATES OF AMERICA, in General Congress, Assembled, appealing to the Supreme Judge of the World for the Rectitude of our Intentions, do, in the Name, and by Authority of the good People of these Colonies, solemnly Publish and Declare, That these United Colonies are, and of Right ought to be, Free and Independent States; that they are absolved from all Allegiance to the British Crown, and that all political Connection between them and the State of Great Britain, is and ought to be totally dissolved; and that as Free and Independent States, they have full Power to levy War, conclude Peace, contract Alliances, establish Commerce, and to do all other Acts and Things which Independent States may of right do. And for the support of this Declaration, with a firm Reliance on the Protection of divine Providence, we mutually pledge to each other our

Lives, our Fortunes and our sacred Honor. Signed by Order and in Behalf of the Congress,

JOHN HANCOCK, President.

Attest.

CHARLES THOMSON, Secretary.

The Constitution of the United States of America

We the People of the United States, in Order to form a more perfect Union, establish Justice, insure domestic Tranquility, provide for the common defence, promote the general Welfare, and secure the Blessings of Liberty to ourselves and our Posterity, do ordain and establish this Constitution for the United States of America.

Article. I.

Section. 1.
All legislative Powers herein granted shall be vested in a Congress of the United States, which shall consist of a Senate and House of Representatives.

Section. 2.
The House of Representatives shall be composed of Members chosen every second Year by the People of the several States, and the Electors in each State shall have the Qualifications requisite for Electors of the most numerous Branch of the State Legislature. No Person shall be a Representative who shall not have attained to the Age of twenty-five Years, and been seven Years a Citizen of the United States, and who shall not, when elected, be an Inhabitant of that State in which he shall be chosen.

Representatives and direct Taxes shall be apportioned among the several States which may be included within this Union, according to their respective Numbers, which shall be determined by adding to the whole Number of free Persons, including those bound to Service for a Term of Years, and excluding Indians not taxed, three fifths of all other Persons. The actual Enumeration shall be made within three Years after the first Meeting of the Congress of the United States, and within every subsequent Term of ten Years, in such Manner as they shall by Law direct. The Number of Representatives shall not exceed one for every thirty Thousand, but each State shall have at Least one Representative; and until such enumeration shall be made, the State of New Hampshire shall be entitled to chuse three, Massachusetts eight, Rhode-Island and Providence Plantations one, Connecticut five, New-York six, New Jersey four, Pennsylvania eight, Delaware one, Maryland six, Virginia ten, North Carolina five, South Carolina five, and Georgia three.

When vacancies happen in the Representation from any State, the Executive Authority thereof shall issue Writs of Election to fill such Vacancies.

The House of Representatives shall chuse their Speaker and other Officers; and shall have the sole Power of Impeachment.

Section. 3.

The Senate of the United States shall be composed of two Senators from each State, chosen by the Legislature thereof, for six Years; and each Senator shall have one Vote.

Immediately after they shall be assembled in Consequence of the first Election, they shall be divided as equally as may be into three Classes. The Seats of the Senators of the first Class shall be vacated at the Expiration of the second Year, of the second Class at the Expiration of the fourth Year, and of the third Class at the Expiration of the sixth Year, so that one third may be chosen every second Year; and if Vacancies happen by Resignation, or otherwise, during the Recess of the Legislature of any State, the Executive thereof may make temporary Appointments until the next Meeting of the Legislature, which shall then fill such Vacancies. No Person shall be a Senator who shall not have attained to the Age of thirty Years, and been nine Years a Citizen of the United States, and who shall not, when elected, be an Inhabitant of that State for which he shall be chosen.

The Vice President of the United States shall be President of the Senate, but shall have no Vote, unless they be equally divided.

The Senate shall chuse their other Officers, and also a President pro tempore, in the Absence of the Vice President, or when he shall exercise the Office of President of the United States.

The Senate shall have the sole Power to try all Impeachments. When sitting for that Purpose, they shall be on Oath or Affirmation. When the President of the United States is tried, the Chief Justice shall preside: And no Person shall be convicted without the Concurrence of two thirds of the Members present.

Judgment in Cases of Impeachment shall not extend further than to removal from Office, and disqualification to hold and enjoy any Office of honor, Trust or Profit under the United States: but the Party convicted shall nevertheless be liable and subject to Indictment, Trial, Judgment and Punishment, according to Law.

Section. 4.

The Times, Places and Manner of holding Elections for Senators and Representatives, shall be prescribed in each State by the Legislature thereof; but the Congress may at any time by Law make or alter such Regulations, except as to the Places of chusing Senators.

The Congress shall assemble at least once in every Year, and such Meeting shall be on the first Monday in December, unless they shall by Law appoint a different Day.

Section.5.

Each House shall be the Judge of the Elections, Returns and Qualifications of its own Members, and a Majority of each shall constitute a Quorum to do Business; but a smaller Number may adjourn from day to day, and may be authorized to compel the Attendance of absent Members, in such Manner, and under such Penalties as each House may provide.

Each House may determine the Rules of its Proceedings, punish its Members for disorderly Behaviour, and, with the Concurrence of two thirds, expel a Member. Each House shall keep a Journal of its Proceedings, and from time to time publish the same, excepting such Parts as may in their Judgment require Secrecy; and the Yeas and Nays of the Members of either House on any question shall, at the Desire of one fifth of those Present, be entered on the Journal.

Neither House, during the Session of Congress, shall, without the Consent of the other, adjourn for more than three days, nor to any other Place than that in which the two Houses shall be sitting.

Section. 6.

The Senators and Representatives shall receive a Compensation for their Services, to be ascertained by Law, and paid out of the Treasury of the United States. They shall in all Cases, except Treason, Felony and Breach of the Peace, be privileged from Arrest during their Attendance at the Session of their respective

Houses, and in going to and returning from the same; and for any Speech or Debate in either House, they shall not be questioned in any other Place.

No Senator or Representative shall, during the Time for which he was elected, be appointed to any civil Office under the Authority of the United States, which shall have been created, or the Emoluments whereof shall have been encreased during such time; and no Person holding any Office under the United States, shall be a Member of either House during his Continuance in Office.

Section. 7.
All Bills for raising Revenue shall originate in the House of Representatives; but the Senate may propose or concur with Amendments as on other Bills.

Every Bill which shall have passed the House of Representatives and the Senate, shall, before it become a Law, be presented to the President of the United States; If he approve he shall sign it, but if not he shall return it, with his Objections to that House in which it shall have originated, who shall enter the Objections at large on their Journal, and proceed to reconsider it. If after such Reconsideration two thirds of that House shall agree to pass the Bill, it shall be sent, together with the Objections, to the other House, by which it shall likewise be reconsidered, and if approved by two thirds of that House, it shall become a Law. But in all such Cases the Votes of both Houses shall be determined by yeas and Nays, and the Names of the Persons voting for and against the Bill shall be entered on the Journal of each House respectively. If any Bill shall not be returned by the President within ten Days (Sundays excepted) after it shall have been presented to him, the Same shall be a Law, in like Manner as if he had signed it, unless the Congress by their Adjournment prevent its Return, in which Case it shall not be a Law.

Every Order, Resolution, or Vote to which the Concurrence of the Senate and House of Representatives may be necessary (except on a question of Adjournment) shall be presented to the President of the United States; and before the Same shall take Effect, shall be approved by him, or being disapproved by him, shall be repassed by two thirds of the Senate and House of Representatives, according to the Rules and Limitations prescribed in the Case of a Bill.

Section. 8.
The Congress shall have Power To lay and collect Taxes, Duties, Imposts and Excises, to pay the Debts and provide for the common Defence and general Welfare of the United States; but all Duties, Imposts and Excises shall be uniform throughout the United States;

To borrow Money on the credit of the United States;

To regulate Commerce with foreign Nations, and among the several States, and with the Indian Tribes; To establish an uniform Rule of Naturalization, and uniform Laws on the subject of Bankruptcies throughout the United States;

To coin Money, regulate the Value thereof, and of foreign Coin, and fix the Standard of Weights and Measures;

To provide for the Punishment of counterfeiting the Securities and current Coin of the United States;

To establish Post Offices and post Roads;

To promote the Progress of Science and useful Arts, by securing for limited Times to Authors and Inventors the exclusive Right to their respective Writings and Discoveries;

To constitute Tribunals inferior to the supreme Court;

To define and punish Piracies and Felonies committed on the high Seas, and Offences against the Law of Nations;

To declare War, grant Letters of Marque and Reprisal, and make Rules concerning Captures on Land and Water;

To raise and support Armies, but no Appropriation of Money to that Use shall be for a longer Term than two Years;

To provide and maintain a Navy;

To make Rules for the Government and Regulation of the land and naval Forces; To provide for calling forth the Militia to execute the Laws of the Union, suppress Insurrections and repel Invasions;

To provide for organizing, arming, and disciplining, the Militia, and for governing such Part of them as may be employed in the Service of the United States, reserving to the States respectively, the Appointment of the Officers, and the Authority of training the Militia according to the discipline prescribed by Congress;

To exercise exclusive Legislation in all Cases whatsoever, over such District (not exceeding ten Miles square) as may, by Cession of particular States, and the Acceptance of Congress, become the Seat of the Government of the United States, and to exercise like Authority over all Places purchased by the Consent of the Legislature of the State in which the Same shall be, for the Erection of Forts, Magazines, Arsenals, dock-Yards, and other needful Buildings; And

To make all Laws which shall be necessary and proper for carrying into Execution the foregoing Powers, and all other Powers vested by this Constitution in the Government of the United States, or in any Department or Officer thereof.

Section. 9.

The Migration or Importation of such Persons as any of the States now existing shall think proper to admit, shall not be prohibited by the Congress prior to the Year one thousand eight hundred and eight, but a Tax or duty may be imposed on such Importation, not exceeding ten dollars for each Person.

The Privilege of the Writ of Habeas Corpus shall not be suspended, unless when in Cases of Rebellion or Invasion the public Safety may require it.

No Bill of Attainder or ex post facto Law shall be passed. No Capitation, or other direct, Tax shall be laid, unless in Proportion to the Census or enumeration herein before directed to be taken.

No Tax or Duty shall be laid on Articles exported from any State.

No Preference shall be given by any Regulation of Commerce or Revenue to the Ports of one State over those of another: nor shall Vessels bound to, or from, one State, be obliged to enter, clear, or pay Duties in another.

No Money shall be drawn from the Treasury, but in Consequence of Appropriations made by Law; and a regular Statement and Account of the Receipts and Expenditures of all public Money shall be published from time to time.

No Title of Nobility shall be granted by the United States: And no Person holding any Office of Profit or Trust under them, shall, without the Consent of the Congress, accept of any present, Emolument, Office, or Title, of any kind whatever, from any King, Prince, or foreign State.

Section. 10.
No State shall enter into any Treaty, Alliance, or Confederation; grant Letters of Marque and Reprisal;

coin Money; emit Bills of Credit; make any Thing but gold and silver Coin a Tender in Payment of Debts; pass any Bill of Attainder, ex post facto Law, or Law impairing the Obligation of Contracts, or grant any Title of Nobility.

No State shall, without the Consent of the Congress, lay any Imposts or Duties on Imports or Exports, except what may be absolutely necessary for executing it's inspection Laws: and the net Produce of all Duties and Imposts, laid by any State on Imports or Exports, shall be for the Use of the Treasury of the United States; and all such Laws shall be subject to the Revision and Controul of the Congress.

No State shall, without the Consent of Congress, lay any Duty of Tonnage, keep Troops, or Ships of War in time of Peace, enter into any Agreement or Compact with another State, or with a foreign Power, or engage in War, unless actually invaded, or in such imminent Danger as will not admit of delay.

Article. II.

Section. 1.
The executive Power shall be vested in a President of the United States of America. He shall hold his Office during the Term of four Years, and, together with the Vice President, chosen for the same Term, be elected, as follows Each State shall appoint, in such Manner as the Legislature thereof may direct, a Number of Electors,

equal to the whole Number of Senators and Representatives to which the State may be entitled in the Congress: but no Senator or Representative, or Person holding an Office of Trust or Profit under the United States, shall be appointed an Elector.

The Electors shall meet in their respective States, and vote by Ballot for two Persons, of whom one at least shall not be an Inhabitant of the same State with themselves. And they shall make a List of all the Persons voted for, and of the Number of Votes for each; which List they shall sign and certify, and transmit sealed to the Seat of the Government of the United States, directed to the President of the Senate. The President of the Senate shall, in the Presence of the Senate and House of Representatives, open all the Certificates, and the Votes shall then be counted. The Person having the greatest Number of Votes shall be the President, if such Number be a Majority of the whole Number of Electors appointed; and if there be more than one who have such Majority, and have an equal Number of Votes, then the House of Representatives shall immediately chuse by Ballot one of them for President; and if no Person have a Majority, then from the five highest on the List the said House shall in like Manner chuse the President. But in chusing the President, the Votes shall be taken by States, the Representation from each State having one Vote; A quorum for this Purpose shall consist of a Member or Members from two thirds of the States, and a Majority of all the States shall be necessary to a Choice. In every

Case, after the Choice of the President, the Person having the greatest Number of Votes of the Electors shall be the Vice President. But if there should remain two or more who have greatest Number of Votes of the Electors shall be the Vice President. But if there should remain two or more who have equal Votes, the Senate shall chuse from them by Ballot the Vice President.

The Congress may determine the Time of chusing the Electors, and the Day on which they shall give their Votes; which Day shall be the same throughout the United States.

No Person except a natural born Citizen, or a Citizen of the United States, at the time of the Adoption of this Constitution, shall be eligible to the Office of President; neither shall any Person be eligible to that Office who shall not have attained to the Age of thirty-five Years, and been fourteen Years a Resident within the United States.

In Case of the Removal of the President from Office, or of his Death, Resignation, or Inability to discharge the Powers and Duties of the said Office, the Same shall devolve on the Vice President, and the Congress may by Law provide for the Case of Removal, Death, Resignation or Inability, both of the President and Vice President, declaring what Officer shall then act as President, and such Officer shall act accordingly, until the Disability be removed, or a President shall be elected.

The President shall, at stated Times, receive for his Services, a Compensation, which shall neither be encreased nor diminished during the Period for which he shall have been elected, and he shall not receive within that Period any other Emolument from the United States, or any of them.

Before he enter on the Execution of his Office, he shall take the following Oath or Affirmation:—"I do solemnly swear (or affirm) that I will faithfully execute the Office of President of the United States, and will to the best of my Ability, preserve, protect and defend the Constitution of the United States."

Section. 2.
The President shall be Commander in Chief of the Army and Navy of the United States, and of the Militia of the several States, when called into the actual Service of the United States; he may require the Opinion, in writing, of the principal Officer in each of the executive Departments, upon any Subject relating to the Duties of their respective Offices, and he shall have Power to grant Reprieves and Pardons for Offences against the United States, except in Cases of Impeachment.

He shall have Power, by and with the Advice and Consent of the Senate, to make Treaties, provided two thirds of the Senators present concur; and he shall nominate, and by and with the Advice and Consent of the Senate, shall appoint Ambassadors, other public Ministers and Consuls, Judges of the supreme Court, and all other Officers of the United States, whose Appointments are not herein otherwise provided for, and which shall be established by Law: but the Congress may by Law vest the Appointment of such inferior Officers, as they think proper, in the President alone, in the Courts of Law, or in the Heads of Departments.

The President shall have Power to fill up all Vacancies that may happen during the Recess of the Senate, by granting Commissions which shall expire at the End of their next Session.

Section. 3.
He shall from time to time give to the Congress Information of the State of the Union, and recommend to their Consideration such Measures as he shall judge necessary and expedient; he may, on extraordinary Occasions, convene both Houses, or either of them, and in Case of Disagreement between them, with Respect to the Time of Adjournment, he may adjourn them to such Time as he shall think proper; he shall receive Ambassadors and other public Ministers; he shall take Care that the Laws be faithfully executed, and shall Commission all the Officers of the United States.

Section. 4.
The President, Vice President and all civil Officers of the United States, shall be removed from Office on Impeachment for, and Conviction of, Treason, Bribery, or other high Crimes and Misdemeanors.

Article. III.

Section. 1.
The judicial Power of the United States, shall be vested in one supreme Court, and in such inferior Courts as the Congress may from time to time ordain and establish. The Judges, both of the supreme and inferior Courts, shall hold their Offices during good Behaviour, and shall, at stated Times, receive for their Services, a Compensation, which shall not be diminished during their Continuance in Office.

Section. 2.
The judicial Power shall extend to all Cases, in Law and Equity, arising under this Constitution, the Laws of the United States, and Treaties made, or which shall be made, under their Authority;—to all Cases affecting Ambassadors, other public Ministers and Consuls;—to all Cases of admiralty and maritime Party;—to Controversies between two or more States;— between a State and Citizens of another State,—between Citizens of different States,—between Citizens of the same State claiming Lands under Grants of different States, and between a State, or the Citizens thereof, and foreign States, Citizens or Subjects.

In all Cases affecting Ambassadors, other public Ministers and Consuls, and those in which a State shall be Party, the supreme Court shall have original Jurisdiction. In all the other Cases before mentioned, the supreme Court shall have appellate Jurisdiction, both as to Law and Fact, with such Exceptions, and under such Regulations as the Congress shall make.

The Trial of all Crimes, except in Cases of Impeachment, shall be by Jury; and such Trial shall be held in the State where the said Crimes shall have been committed; but when not committed within any State, the Trial shall be at such Place or Places as the Congress may by Law have directed.

Section. 3.

Treason against the United States, shall consist only in levying War against them, or in adhering to their Enemies, giving them Aid and Comfort. No Person shall be convicted of Treason unless on the Testimony of two Witnesses to the same overt Act, or on Confession in open Court.

The Congress shall have Power to declare the Punishment of Treason, but no Attainder of Treason shall work Corruption of Blood, or Forfeiture except during the Life of the Person attainted.

Article. IV.

Section. 1.

Full Faith and Credit shall be given in each State to the public Acts, Records, and judicial Proceedings of every other State. And the Congress may by general Laws prescribe the Manner in which such Acts, Records and Proceedings shall be proved, and the Effect thereof.

Section. 2.

The Citizens of each State shall be entitled to all Privileges and Immunities of Citizens in the several States.

A Person charged in any State with Treason, Felony, or other Crime, who shall flee from Justice, and be found in another State, shall on Demand of the executive Authority of the State from which he fled, be delivered up, to be removed to the State having Jurisdiction of the Crime.

No Person held to Service or Labour in one State, under the Laws thereof, escaping into another, shall, in Consequence of any Law or Regulation therein, be discharged from such Service or Labour, but shall be delivered up on Claim of the Party to whom such Service or Labour may be due.

Section. 3.

New States may be admitted by the Congress into this Union; but no new State shall be formed or erected within the Jurisdiction of any other State; nor any State be formed by the Junction of two or more States, or Parts of States, without the Consent of the Legislatures of the States concerned as well as of the Congress. The Congress shall have Power to dispose of and make all needful Rules and Regulations respecting the Territory or other Property belonging to the United States; and nothing in this Constitution shall be so construed as to

Prejudice any Claims of the United States, or of any particular State.

Section. 4.

The United States shall guarantee to every State in this Union a Republican Form of Government, and shall protect each of them against Invasion; and on Application of the Legislature, or of the Executive (when the Legislature cannot be convened) against domestic Violence.

Article. V.

The Congress, whenever two thirds of both Houses shall deem it necessary, shall propose Amendments to this Constitution, or, on the Application of the Legislatures of two thirds of the several States, shall call a Convention for proposing Amendments, which, in either Case, shall be valid to all Intents and Purposes, as Part of this Constitution, when ratified by the Legislatures of three fourths of the several States, or by Conventions in three fourths thereof, as the one or the other Mode of Ratification may be proposed by the Congress; Provided that no Amendment which may be made prior to the Year One thousand eight hundred and eight shall in any Manner affect the first and fourth Clauses in the Ninth Section of the first Article; and that no State, without its Consent, shall be deprived of its equal Suffrage in the Senate.

Article. VI.

All Debts contracted and Engagements entered into, before the Adoption of this Constitution, shall be as valid against the United States under this Constitution, as under the Confederation.

This Constitution, and the Laws of the United States which shall be made in Pursuance thereof; and all Treaties made, or which shall be made, under the Authority of the United States, shall be the supreme Law of the Land; and the Judges in every State shall be bound thereby, any Thing in the Constitution or Laws of any State to the Contrary notwithstanding. The Senators and Representatives before mentioned, and the Members of the several State Legislatures, and all executive and judicial Officers, both of the United States and of the several States, shall be bound by Oath or Affirmation, to support this Constitution; but no religious Test shall ever be required as a Qualification to any Office or public Trust under the United States.

Article. VII.

The Ratification of the Conventions of nine States, shall be sufficient for the Establishment of this Constitution between the States so ratifying the Same. The Word, "the," being interlined between the seventh and eighth

Lines of the first Page, The Word "Thirty" being partly written on an Erazure in the fifteenth Line of the first Page, The Words "is tried" being interlined between the thirty second and thirty third Lines of the first Page and the Word "the" being interlined between the forty third and forty fourth Lines of the second Page.

Attest William Jackson Secretary

Done in Convention by the Unanimous Consent of the States present the Seventeenth Day of September in the Year of our Lord one thousand seven hundred and Eighty-seven and of the Independance of the United States of America the Twelfth. In witness whereof We have hereunto subscribed our Names,

G°. Washington
Presidt and deputy from Virginia

THE AMENDMENTS TO THE CONSTITUTION OF THE UNITED STATES of AMERICA AS RATIFIED BY THE STATES

Preamble to the Bill of Rights
Congress of the United States begun and held at the City of New-York, on Wednesday the fourth of March, one thousand seven hundred and eighty-nine.

THE Conventions of a number of the States, having at the time of their adopting the Constitution, expressed a desire, in order to prevent misconstruction or abuse of its powers, that further declaratory and restrictive clauses should be added: And as extending the ground of public confidence in the Government, will best ensure the beneficent ends of its institution. RESOLVED by the Senate and House of Representatives of the United States of America, in Congress assembled, two thirds of both Houses concurring, that the following Articles be proposed to the Legislatures of the several States, as amendments to the Constitution of the United States, all, or any of which Articles, when ratified by three fourths of the said Legislatures, to be valid to all intents and purposes, as part of the said Constitution; viz.

ARTICLES in addition to, and Amendment of the Constitution of the United States of America, proposed by Congress, and ratified by the Legislatures of the several States, pursuant to the fifth Article of the original Constitution.

(Note: The first 10 amendments to the Constitution were ratified December 15, 1791, and form what is known as the "**Bill of Rights.**")

Amendment I.

Congress shall make no law respecting an establishment of religion, or prohibiting the free exercise thereof; or abridging the freedom of speech, or of the press, or the right of the people peaceably to assemble, and to petition the Government for a redress of grievances.

Amendment II.

A well-regulated Militia, being necessary to the security of a free State, the right of the people to keep and bear Arms, shall not be infringed.

Amendment III.

No Soldier shall, in time of peace be quartered in any house, without the consent of the Owner, nor in time of war, but in a manner to be prescribed by law.

Amendment IV.

The right of the people to be secure in their persons, houses, papers, and effects, against unreasonable searches and seizures, shall not be violated, and no Warrants shall issue, but upon probable cause, supported by Oath or affirmation, and particularly describing the place to be searched, and the persons or things to be seized.

Amendment V.

No person shall be held to answer for a capital, or otherwise infamous crime, unless on a presentment or indictment of a Grand Jury, except in cases arising in the land or naval forces, or in the Militia, when in actual service in time of War or public danger; nor shall any person be subject for the same offence to be twice put in jeopardy of life or limb; nor shall be compelled in any criminal case to be a witness against himself, nor be deprived of life, liberty, or property, without due process of law; nor shall private property be taken for public use, without just compensation.

Amendment VI.

In all criminal prosecutions, the accused shall enjoy the right to a speedy and public trial, by an impartial jury of the State and district wherein the crime shall have been committed, which district shall have been previously ascertained by law, and to be informed of the nature and cause of the accusation; to be confronted with the witnesses against him; to have compulsory process for obtaining witnesses in his favor, and to have the Assistance of Counsel for his for public use, without just compensation.

Amendment VII.

In suits at common law, where the value in controversy shall exceed twenty dollars, the right of trial by jury shall be preserved, and no fact tried by a jury shall be otherwise re-examined in any Court of the United States, than according to the rules of the common law.

Amendment VIII.

Excessive bail shall not be required, nor excessive fines imposed, nor cruel and unusual punishments inflicted.

Amendment IX.

The enumeration in the Constitution, of certain rights, shall not be construed to deny or disparage others retained by the people.

Amendment X.

The powers not delegated to the United States by the Constitution, nor prohibited by it to the States, are reserved to the States respectively, or to the people.

Amendment XI.

Passed by Congress March 4, 1794. Ratified February 7, 1795. (Note: A portion of Article III, Section 2 of the Constitution was modified by the 11th Amendment.)

The Judicial power of the United States shall not be construed to extend to any suit in law or equity, commenced or prosecuted against one of the United States by Citizens of another State, or by Citizens or Subjects of any Foreign State.

Amendment XII.

Passed by Congress December 9, 1803. Ratified June 15, 1804. (Note: A portion of Article II, Section 1 of the Constitution was changed by the 12th Amendment.)

The Electors shall meet in their respective states, and vote by ballot for President and Vice-President, one of whom, at least, shall not be an inhabitant of the same state with themselves; they shall name in their ballots the person voted for as President, and in distinct ballots the person voted for as Vice-President, and they shall make distinct lists of all persons voted for as President, and of all persons voted for as Vice-President, and of the number of votes for each, which lists they shall sign and certify, and transmit sealed to the seat of the government of the United States, directed to the President of the Senate;-the President of the Senate shall, in the presence of the Senate and House of Representatives, open all the certificates and the votes shall then be counted;-The person having the greatest number of votes for President, shall be the President, if such number be a majority of the whole number of Electors appointed; and if no person have such majority, then from the persons having the highest numbers not exceeding three on the list of those voted for as President, the House of Representatives shall choose

161

immediately, by ballot, the President. But in choosing the President, the votes shall be taken by states, the representation from each state having one vote; a quorum for this purpose shall consist of a member or members from two-thirds of the states, and a majority of all the states shall be necessary to a choice. [And if the House of Representatives shall not choose a President whenever the right of choice shall devolve upon them, before the fourth day of March next following, then the Vice-President shall act as President, as in case of the death or other constitutional disability of the President.]* The person having the greatest number of votes as Vice-President, shall be the Vice-President, if such number be a majority of the whole number of Electors appointed, and if no person have a majority, then from the two highest numbers on the list, the Senate shall choose the Vice-President; a quorum for the purpose shall consist of two-thirds of the whole number of Senators, and a majority of the whole number shall be necessary to a choice. But no person constitutionally ineligible to the office of President shall be eligible to that of Vice-President of the United States.

*Superseded by Section 3 of the 20th Amendment.

Amendment XIII.

Passed by Congress January 31, 1865. Ratified December 6, 1865. (Note: A portion of Article IV, Section 2 of the Constitution was changed by the 13th Amendment.)

SECTION 1.

Neither slavery nor involuntary servitude, except as a punishment for crime whereof the party shall have been duly convicted, shall exist within the United States, or any place subject to their jurisdiction.

SECTION 2.

Congress shall have power to enforce this article by appropriate legislation.

Amendment XIV.

Passed by Congress June 13, 1866. Ratified July 9, 1868. (Note: Article I, Section 2 of the Constitution was modified by Section 2 of the 14th Amendment.)

SECTION 1.

All persons born or naturalized in the United States and subject to the jurisdiction thereof, are citizens of the United States and of the State wherein they reside. No State shall make or enforce any law which shall abridge the privileges or immunities of citizens of the United States; nor shall any State deprive any person of life, liberty, or property, without due process of law; nor deny to any person within its jurisdiction the equal protection of the laws.

SECTION 2.

Representatives shall be apportioned among the several States according to their respective numbers, counting the whole number of persons in each State, excluding Indians not taxed. But when the right to vote at any election for the choice of electors for President and Vice President of the United States, Representatives in Congress, the Executive and Judicial officers of a State, or the members of the Legislature thereof, is denied to any of the male inhabitants of such State, [being twenty-one years of age,]* and citizens of the United States, or in any way abridged, except for participation in rebellion, or other crime, the basis of representation therein shall be reduced in the proportion which the number of such male citizens shall bear to the whole number of male citizens twenty-one years of age in such State.

SECTION 3.

No person shall be a Senator or Representative in Congress, or elector of President and Vice President, or hold any office, civil or military, under the United States, or under any State, who, having previously taken an oath, as a member of Congress, or as an officer of the United States, or as a member of any State legislature, or as an executive or judicial officer of any State, to support the Constitution of the United States, shall have engaged in insurrection or rebellion against the same, or given aid or comfort to the enemies thereof. But Congress may by a vote of two-thirds of each House, remove such disability.

SECTION 4.

The validity of the public debt of the United States, authorized by law, including debts incurred for payment of pensions and bounties for services in suppressing insurrection or rebellion, shall not be questioned. But neither the United States nor any State shall assume or pay any debt or obligation incurred in aid of insurrection or rebellion against the United States, or any claim for the loss or emancipation of any slave; but all such debts, obligations and claims shall be held illegal and void.

SECTION 5.

The Congress shall have the power to enforce, by appropriate legislation, the provisions of this article.   *Changed by Section 1 of the 26th Amendment.

Amendment XV.

Passed by Congress February 26, 1869. Ratified February 3, 1870.

SECTION 1.

The right of citizens of the United States to vote shall not be denied or abridged by the United States or by any State on account of race, color, or previous condition of servitude.

SECTION 2.

The Congress shall have the power to enforce this article by appropriate legislation.

Amendment XVI.

Passed by Congress July 2, 1909. Ratified February 3, 1913. (Note: Article I, Section 9 of the Constitution was modified by the 16th Amendment.)

The Congress shall have power to lay and collect taxes on incomes, from whatever source derived, without apportionment among the several States, and without regard to any census or enumeration.

Amendment XVII.

Passed by Congress May 13, 1912. Ratified April

8, 1913.

(Note: Article I, Section 3 of the Constitution was modified by the 17th Amendment.)

The Senate of the United States shall be composed of two Senators from each State, elected by the people thereof, for six years; and each Senator shall have one vote. The electors in each State shall have the qualifications requisite for electors of the most numerous branch of the State legislatures.

When vacancies happen in the representation of any State in the Senate, the executive authority of such State shall issue writs of election to fill such vacancies: Provided, That the legislature of any State may empower the executive thereof to make temporary appointments until the people fill the vacancies by election as the legislature may direct.

This amendment shall not be so construed as to affect the election or term of any Senator chosen before it becomes valid as part of the Constitution.

Amendment XVIII.
Passed by Congress December 18, 1917. Ratified January 16, 1919. Repealed by the 21st Amendment, December 5, 1933.

SECTION 1.

After one year from the ratification of this article the manufacture, sale, or transportation of intoxicating liquors within, the importation thereof into, or the exportation thereof from the United States and all territory subject to the jurisdiction thereof for beverage purposes is hereby prohibited.

SECTION 2.

The Congress and the several States shall have concurrent power to enforce this article by appropriate legislation.

SECTION 3.

This article shall be inoperative unless it shall have been ratified as an amendment to the Constitution by the legislatures of the several States, as provided in the Constitution, within seven years from the date of the submission hereof to the States by the Congress.

Amendment XIX.

Passed by Congress June 4, 1919. Ratified August 18, 1920.

The right of citizens of the United States to vote shall not be denied or abridged by the United States or by any State on account of sex. Congress shall have power to enforce this article by appropriate legislation.

Passed by Congress March 2, 1932. Ratified January 23, 1933. (Note: Article I, Section 4 of the Constitution was modified by Section 2 of this Amendment. In addition, a portion of the 12th Amendment was superseded by Section 3.)

SECTION 1.

The terms of the President and the Vice President shall end at noon on the 20th day of January, and the terms of Senators and Representatives at noon on the 3d day of January, of the years in which such terms would have ended if this article had not been ratified; and the terms of their successors shall then begin.

SECTION 2.

The Congress shall assemble at least once in every year, and such meeting shall begin at noon on the 3d day of January, unless they shall by law appoint a different day.

SECTION 3.

If, at the time fixed for the beginning of the term of the President, the President elect shall have died, the Vice President elect shall become President. If a President shall not have been chosen before the time fixed for the beginning of his term, or if the President elect shall have failed to qualify, then the Vice President elect shall act as President until a President shall have qualified; and the Congress may by law provide for the case wherein neither a President elect nor a Vice President shall have qualified, declaring who shall then act as President, or the manner in which one who is to act shall be selected, and such person shall act accordingly until a President or Vice President shall have qualified.

SECTION 4.

The Congress may by law provide for the case of the death of any of the persons from whom the House of Representatives may choose a President whenever the right of choice shall have devolved upon them, and for the case of the death of any of the persons from whom the Senate may choose a Vice President whenever the right of choice shall have devolved upon them.

SECTION 5.

Sections 1 and 2 shall take effect on the 15th day of October following the ratification of this article.

SECTION 6.

This article shall be inoperative unless it shall have been ratified as an amendment to the Constitution by the legislatures of three-fourths of the several States within seven years from the date of its submission.

Amendment XXI.

Passed by Congress February 20, 1933. Ratified December 5, 1933.

SECTION 1.

The eighteenth article of amendment to the Constitution of the United States is hereby repealed.

SECTION 2.

The transportation or importation into any State, Territory, or possession of the United States for delivery or use therein of intoxicating liquors, in violation of the laws thereof, is hereby prohibited.

SECTION 3.

This article shall be inoperative unless it shall have been ratified as an amendment to the Constitution by conventions in the several States, as provided in the Constitution, within seven years from the date of the submission hereof to the States by the Congress.

Amendment XXII.

Passed by Congress March 21, 1947. Ratified February 27, 1951.

SECTION 1.

No person shall be elected to the office of the President more than twice, and no person who has held the office of President, or acted as President, for more than two years of a term to which some other person was elected President shall be elected to the office of President more than once. But this Article shall not apply to any person holding the office of President when this Article was proposed by Congress, and shall not prevent any person who may be holding the office of President, or acting as President, during the term within which this Article becomes operative from holding the office of President or acting as President during the remainder of such term.

SECTION 2.

This article shall be inoperative unless it shall have been ratified as an amendment to the Constitution by the legislatures of three-fourths of the several States within seven years from the date of its submission to the States by the Congress.

Amendment XXIII.

Passed by Congress June 16, 1960. Ratified March 29, 1961.

SECTION 1.

The District constituting the seat of Government of the United States shall appoint in such manner as Congress may direct:

A number of electors of President and Vice President equal to the whole number of Senators and Representatives in Congress to which the District would be entitled if it were a State, but in no event more than the least populous State; they shall be in addition to those appointed by the States, but they shall be considered, for the purposes of the election of President and Vice President, to be electors

appointed by a State; and they shall meet in the District and perform such duties as provided by the twelfth article of amendment.

SECTION 2.

The Congress shall have power to enforce this article by appropriate legislation.

Amendment XXIV.

Passed by Congress August 27, 1962. Ratified January 23, 1964.

SECTION 1.

The right of citizens of the United States to vote in any primary or other election for President or Vice President, for electors for President or Vice President, or for Senator or Representative in Congress, shall not be denied or abridged by the United States or any State by reason of failure to pay poll tax or other tax.

SECTION 2.

The Congress shall have power to enforce this article by appropriate legislation.

Amendment XXV.

Passed by Congress July 6, 1965. Ratified February 10, 1967

SECTION   **1.**
In case of the removal of the President from office or of his death or resignation, the Vice President shall become President.

SECTION 2.

Whenever there is a vacancy in the office of the Vice President, the President shall nominate a Vice President who shall take office upon confirmation by a majority vote of both Houses of Congress.

SECTION 3.

Whenever the President transmits to the President pro tempore of the Senate and the Speaker of the House of Representatives his written declaration that he is unable to discharge the powers and duties of his office, and until he transmits to them a written declaration to the contrary, such powers and duties shall be discharged by the Vice President as Acting President.

174

SECTION 4.

Whenever the Vice President and a majority of either the principal officers of the executive departments or of such other body as Congress may by law provide, transmit to the President pro tempore of the Senate and the Speaker of the House of Representatives their written declaration that the President is unable to discharge the powers and duties of his office, the Vice President shall immediately assume the powers and duties of the office as Acting President.

Thereafter, when the President transmits to the President pro tempore of the Senate and the Speaker of the House of Representatives his written declaration that no inability exists, he shall resume the powers and duties of his office unless the Vice President and a majority of either the principal officers of the executive department or of such other body as Congress may by law provide, transmit within four days to the President pro tempore of the Senate and the Speaker of the House of Representatives their written declaration that the President is unable to discharge the powers and duties of his office. Thereupon Congress shall decide the issue, assembling within forty-eight hours for that purpose if not in session. If the Congress, within twenty-one days after receipt of the latter written declaration, or, if Congress is not in session, within twenty-one days after

Congress is required to assemble, determines by two-thirds vote of both Houses that the President is unable to discharge the powers and duties of his office, the Vice President shall continue to discharge the same as Acting President; otherwise, the President shall resume the powers and duties of his office.

Amendment XXVI.

Passed by Congress March 23, 1971. Ratified July 1, 1971.

SECTION 1.

The right of citizens of the United States, who are eighteen years of age or older, to vote shall not be denied or abridged by the United States or by any State on account of age.

SECTION 2.

The Congress shall have power to enforce this article by appropriate legislation.

Amendment XXVII.

Passed by Congress September 25, 1789. Ratified May 5, 1992.

No law, varying the compensation for the services of the Senators and Representatives, shall take effect, until an election of Representatives shall have intervened.

Conclusions about the Good Life

I hope you will keep this little book conveniently at hand and refer to it often. When on occasion I am ashamed of something I have done (or as often failed to do), it is usually because I failed to remember and exemplify one of these principles that we have discussed. I trust you will do better.

At several points in our discussion I have recapitulated some of the more critical truths (and sections), hence it would be overkill for me to do that now. Instead, I'll try and describe in a more general sense the strategy we are pursuing and hope this effort will clarify the discrete values and behavioral tactics that I am recommending and the peace such a life brings.

The Greek philosopher Socrates said the unexamined life is not worth living. That is to say, the accomplishments of a life well lived do not happen accidentally. It will only come from thinking carefully about what the good life entails, what one wants the sum of his life to be, and disciplined purposeful living each day. Have you thought about that? Did you use objective criteria or only your personal and momentary preference? Have you decided that you need to make changes? Are you following through with those resolutions?

I am certainly not saying one should follow a harsh, monastic life devoid of all beauty and pleasure, but our life must be guided by a reliable moral compass and not squandered on whims and amusement if it is to have enduring value for us, our families, and peers. If that be so, one must determine what will be the source of that moral authority in one's life, the One who says we should, or ought, to behave in a certain way.

For decades humanist skeptics have argued against a universal moral imperative, asserting that those of us who insist some things should be done, and others ought not be done, are casting blame on others, causing them needlessly to feel guilty. I find several problems with this argument. Were there no agreed universal moral imperative (even with variation in some details), then we would each be left with our own opinions and preferences, there would be no common values to mediate between us, and we would all be functional sociopaths, exploiting one another to achieve our own ends by all available means. We need a universal moral imperative, and those who would deprive us of it are doing us no favor. To have value for us, that imperative must be expressed in discrete commands and prohibitions that we will follow. Then there is this problem: we do not just feel guilty, we are guilty of violating our own code, and all who have a moral code know that is true. We need help, forgiveness, direction, and a divine source of capacity to live as we know we should.

I believe and have argued above that the best source of that moral authority is the Creator God of the Hebrew and Christian Bible, that He actually exists, that He has given us commands in Holy Scripture, and He will require us to give account for our behavior. Certainly, there are other religions, and some of them hold elements of a moral code in common with Christianity. C.S. Lewis believed that all or most religions contain some valuable truths but that the progressive revelations of Judaism and Christianity give us the culmination and keystone of all Truth in Jesus Christ. The author of the epistle to the Hebrews proclaimed as much in his first sentence and continued to assert it to the last verse. The founders of our nation clearly stated their belief that God, our Creator, delegates authority to human government, but only He has the ultimate authority to direct our lives and determine what is good and desirable both in society, in our families, and in His Church. The Bible is the only reliable source of knowledge available to us concerning the attributes of God (what He is like) and what He wants of us, whom He made to be in many respects like Himself.

Jehovah, or Yahweh, in all of His manifestations is self-sufficient. He does not need us, and we can neither add anything to Him nor detract from Him. Those who embrace Him find great and lasting peace; those who are offended by Him will be shattered and pulverized (Psalm 119:165; Romans 9:33; 1 Peter 2:8). That being the case, although He insists we were made to worship, honor, love, and trust Him, most of His commands and teachings are to direct us in our relationships with other people, and most of our service for God is more immediately serving other people. Hence, the broad principles, "love your neighbor as you love yourself," "treat others as you wish to be treated," "be kind and generous," and, leaving less wiggle room, "do not lie," "do not steal," "do not murder," "do not commit adultery," and "work to provide for your own needs, those of your family, and to be able to help others in need."

We will sometimes fail, and when we do, it is necessary to confess it and ask forgiveness in the appropriate context, forgive others who seek it, and continue on, doing our best but trusting God. To help us in this matter, we need to form trust relationships and specifically have one person or a very small group, probably not more than three, with whom we will be completely transparent, be accountable for our behavior, and receive counsel. It works well when this can be a mutual relationship, with each party making commitments and helping one another.

It is good while we are young to think carefully about the kind of person we want to be, to embrace the principles we have considered above that we choose to guide our behavior, and then seek out one or more responsible and trustworthy friends who share similar values and who are also engaged in this quest to live a good life. Our perception of our own behavior is distorted by our subjectivity, but when we are candid and kind, we can help one another to overcome that handicap, to gain a more accurate perception of ourselves, making corrections when needed, and we can also encourage one another when we are discouraged with our performance. Many years ago, I said to a good friend, "Speak the truth to me, please, and I won't get angry." After some reflection the next time we met I told him, "I may get angry, but I'll get over it," and I need you to help me do my best, to live a good life. I pray you, dear reader, will live a good life that will profit those around you, that will give you a well-deserved sense of satisfaction, and bring our Lord to say, "Well done good and faithful servant."

Important Bible Verses That I Very Much Want You to Know

All of the Bible is God's Word, it is given to us by Him for our instruction and profit but it is so large that many people will not read it all or will do so seldom. Others of us will read it but not remember it all. Below are a few verses from the Bible that are important to me because I believe they should be remembered and guide our behavior each day. I will not include some Scriptures that are very well known and I trust you have learned them from others. Most of those I list give me a particularly valuable insight into the nature of God and His working with humanity, and I cite them because they are quite important but not so commonly known.

Some verses that are well-known because of precious truths they contain:

Romans 3:23: "For all have sinned and fallen short of the glory of God.'

Romans 5:8, 9: "But God demonstrates His own love toward us, in that while we were still sinners, Christ died for us. Much more then, having now been justified by His blood, we shall be saved from wrath through Him."

John 3:16–18: "For God so loved the world that

He gave His only begotten Son, that whoever believes in Him should not perish but have everlasting life. For God did not send His Son into the world to condemn the world, but that the world through Him might be saved. He who believes in Him is not condemned; but he who does not believe is condemned already, because he has not believed in the name of the only begotten Son of God." 1 John 4:7, 8: "Beloved, let us love one another, for love is of God; and everyone who loves is born of God and knows God. He who does not love does not know God, for God is love."

John 1:10–14: "He was in the world, and the world was made through Him, and the world did not know Him. 11 He came to His own, and His own did not receive Him. But as many as received Him, to them He gave the right to become children of God, to those who believe in His name: who were born, not of blood, nor of the will of the flesh, nor of the will of man, but of God. And the Word became flesh and dwelt among us, and we beheld His glory, the glory as of the only begotten of the Father, full of grace and truth."

Romans 6:22, 23: "But now having been set free from sin, and having become slaves of God, you have your fruit to holiness, and the end, everlasting life. For the wages of sin is death, but the gift of God is eternal life in Christ Jesus our Lord."

II Corinthians 5:21: "For He made Him who knew no sin to be sin for us, that we might become the righteousness of God in Him."

Romans 1:16, 17: "For I am not ashamed of the gospel of Christ, for it is the power of God to salvation for everyone who believes, for the Jew first and also for the Greek. 17 For in it the righteousness of God is revealed from faith to faith; as it is written, "The just shall live by faith." [These last five words are found four times in the Bible; that means they are very important.

Romans 10:9–17: "That if you confess with your mouth the Lord Jesus and believe in your heart that God has raised Him from the dead, you will be saved. For with the heart one believes unto righteousness, and with the mouth confession is made unto salvation. For the Scripture says, "Whoever believes on Him will not be put to shame." For there is no distinction between Jew and Greek, for the same Lord over all is rich to all who call upon Him. For "whoever calls on the name of the LORD shall be saved." How then shall they call on Him in whom they have not believed? And how shall they believe in Him of whom they have not heard? And how shall they hear without a preacher? And how shall they preach unless they are sent? As it is written: "How beautiful are the feet of those who preach the gospel of peace, who bring glad tidings of good things!" But they have not all obeyed the gospel. For Isaiah says, "Lord, who has believed our report?" So then faith comes by hearing, and hearing by the word of God. Ephesians 2:8–10: "For by grace you have been saved through faith, and that not of yourselves; it is the gift of God, not of works, lest anyone should boast. For we are His workmanship, created in Christ Jesus for good works, which God prepared beforehand that we should walk in them."

1 Corinthians 2:9–14: "But as it is written: "Eye has not seen, nor ear heard, nor have entered into the heart of man the things which God has prepared for those who love Him." But God has revealed them to us through His Spirit. For the Spirit searches all things, yes, the deep things of God. For what man knows the things of a man except the spirit of the man which is in him? Even so no one knows the things of God except the Spirit of God. Now we have received, not the spirit of the world, but the Spirit who is from God, that we might know the things that have been freely given to us by God. These things we also speak, not in words which man's wisdom teaches but which the Holy Spirit teaches, comparing spiritual things with spiritual. But the natural man does not receive the things of the Spirit

of God, for they are foolishness to him; nor can he know them, because they are spiritually discerned."

1 John 1:6–2:2: "If we say that we have fellowship with Him, and walk in darkness, we lie and do not practice the truth. But if we walk in the light as He is in the light, we have fellowship with one another, and the blood of Jesus Christ His Son cleanses us from all sin. If we say that we have no sin, we deceive ourselves, and the truth is not in us. If we confess our sins, He is faithful and just to forgive us our sins and to cleanse us from all unrighteousness. If we say that we have not sinned, we make Him a liar, and His word is not in us. My little children, these things I write to you, so that you may not sin. And if anyone sins, we have an Advocate with the Father, Jesus Christ the righteous. And He Himself is the propitiation for our sins, and not for ours only but also for the whole world."

Luke 13:3: "I tell you, no; but unless you repent you will all likewise perish."

Acts 3:19: "Repent therefore and be converted, that your sins may be blotted out, so that times of refreshing may come from the presence of the Lord."

Less Commonly Known Verses but Very Important:

Deuteronomy 6:4–7: Hear, O Israel: The LORD our God, the LORD is one! You shall love the LORD your God with all your heart, with all your soul, and with all your strength. And these words which I command you today shall be in your heart. You shall teach them diligently to your children, and shall talk of them when you sit in your house, when you walk by the way, when you lie down, and when you rise up."

Deuteronomy 29:29: "The secret things belong to the LORD our God, but those things which are revealed belong to us and to our children forever, that we may do all the words of this law." [God reveals to us what we need to know, not all we want to know, so we can learn to trust Him and obey. Many, in their proud arrogance, stumble over this.]

Psalm 145:8, 9: "The LORD is gracious and full of compassion, slow to anger and great in mercy. the LORD is good to all, and His tender mercies are over all His works."

Psalm 32:1, 2: "Blessed is he whose transgression is forgiven, whose sin is covered. Blessed is the man to whom the LORD does not impute iniquity and in whose spirit there is no deceit."

Isaiah 43:25: "I, even I, am He who blots out your transgressions for My own sake; and I will not remember your sins."

John 6:37: "All that the Father gives Me will come to Me, and the one who comes to Me I will by no means cast out."

John 15:5: "I am the Vine, you are the branches. He who abides in Me, and I in him, bears much fruit; for without Me you can do nothing."

John 6:44: "No one can come to Me unless the Father who sent Me draws him; and I will raise him up at the last day.

1 John 2:3: "Now by this we know that we know Him, if we keep His commandments."

1 John 3:14: "We know that we have passed from death to life, because we love the brethren. He who does not love his brother abides in death."

1 John 4:13: "By this we know that we abide in Him, and He in us, because He has given us of His Spirit."

Romans 8:15, 16: "For you did not receive the spirit of bondage again to fear, but you received the Spirit of adoption by whom we cry out, "Abba, Father." The Spirit Himself bears witness with our spirit that we are children of God (See also Galatians 4:6.).”

Romans 8:28–39: “And we know that all things work together for good to those who love God, to those who are the called according to His purpose. For whom He foreknew, He also predestined to be conformed to the image of His Son, that He might be the firstborn among many brethren. Moreover, whom He predestined, these He also called; whom He called, these He also justified; and whom He justified, these He also glorified. What then shall we say to these things? If God is for us, who can be against us? He who did not spare His own Son, but delivered Him up for us all, how shall He not with Him also freely give us all things? Who shall bring a charge against God’s elect? It is God who justifies. Who is he who condemns? It is Christ who died, and furthermore is also risen, who is even at the right hand of God, who also makes intercession for us. Who shall separate us from the love of Christ? Shall tribulation, or distress, or persecution, or famine, or nakedness, or peril, or sword? As it is written: “For Your sake we are killed all day long; We are accounted as sheep for the slaughter.” Yet in all these things we are more than conquerors through Him who loved us. For I am persuaded that neither death nor life, nor angels nor principalities nor powers, nor things present nor things to come, nor height nor depth, nor any other created thing, shall be able to separate us from the love of God which is in Christ Jesus our Lord." [Read Romans 11 and don't argue with or accuse God. Bow in humility before the One Who has the right to do as He pleases with us. See also Ephesians 1:5, 9.]

Genesis 1:1: "In the beginning God created the heavens and the earth."

John 1:1–3: "In the beginning was the Word, and the Word was with God, and the Word was God. He was in the beginning with God. All things were made through Him, and without Him nothing was made that was made."

John 14:9: "Jesus said to him, "Have I been with you so long, and yet you have not known Me, Philip? He who has seen Me has seen the Father; so how can you say, 'Show us the Father?'" [Read these next two passages carefully and you will see the sovereignty of GOD and His instrumentality in the responsibility and utility of man in the same verses.]

Genesis 18:18, 19: "Since Abraham shall surely become a great and mighty nation, and all the nations of the earth shall be blessed in him? For I have known him, in order that he may command his children and his household after him, that they keep the way of the LORD, to do righteousness and justice, that the LORD may bring to Abraham what He has spoken to him."

2 Timothy 2:10: "Therefore I endure all things for the sake of the elect, that they also may obtain the salvation which is in Christ Jesus with eternal glory.

Exodus 15:11: "Who is like You, O LORD, among the gods? Who is like You, glorious in holiness, fearful in praises, doing wonders?"

The Ten Commandments (Exodus 20:1–17): "And God spoke all these words, saying: "I am the LORD your God, who brought you out of the land of Egypt, out of the house of bondage. You shall have no other gods before Me. You shall not make for yourself a carved image, or any likeness of anything that is in heaven above, or that is in the earth beneath, or that is in the water under the earth; you shall not bow down to them nor serve them. For I, the LORD your God, am a jealous God, visiting the iniquity of the fathers on the children to the third and fourth generations of those who hate Me, but showing mercy to thousands, to those who love Me and keep My commandments. "You shall not take the name of the LORD your God in vain, for the LORD will not hold him guiltless who takes His name in vain. "Remember the Sabbath day, to keep it holy. Six days you shall labor and do all your work, but the seventh day is the Sabbath of the LORD your God. In it you shall do no work: you, nor your son, nor your daughter, nor your male servant, nor your female servant, nor your cattle, nor your stranger who is within your gates. For in six days the LORD made the heavens and the earth, the sea, and all that is in them, and rested the seventh day. Therefore, the LORD blessed the Sabbath day and hallowed it. "Honor your father and your mother, that your days may be long upon the land which the LORD your God is giving you. "You shall not murder. "You shall not commit adultery. "You shall not steal. "You shall not bear false witness against your neighbor. "You shall not covet your neighbor's house; you shall not covet your neighbor's wife, nor his male servant, nor his female servant, nor his ox, nor his donkey, nor anything that is your neighbor's."

The Beatitudes; the Charter of Christ's Kingdom

(Matthew 5:1–12): "And seeing the multitudes, He went up on a mountain, and when He was seated His disciples came to Him. Then He opened His mouth and taught them, saying: "Blessed are the poor in spirit, for theirs is the kingdom of heaven. Blessed are those who mourn, for they shall be comforted. Blessed are the meek, for they shall inherit the earth. Blessed are those who hunger and thirst for righteousness, for they shall be filled. Blessed are the merciful, for they shall obtain mercy. Blessed are the pure in heart, for they shall see God. Blessed are the peacemakers, for they shall be called sons of God. Blessed are those who are persecuted for righteousness' sake, for theirs is the kingdom of heaven. Blessed are you when they revile and persecute you, and say all kinds of evil against you falsely for My sake. Rejoice and be exceedingly glad, for great is your reward in heaven, for so they persecuted the prophets who were before you."

Psalms 119:165: "Great peace have those who love Your law, and nothing causes them to stumble."

Ecclesiastes 8:11: "Because sentence against an evil work is not executed speedily, therefore the heart of the sons of men is fully set in them to do evil.

Lamentations 3:21–27: "This I recall to my mind, therefore I have hope; through the LORD's mercies we are not consumed, because His compassions fail not. They are new every morning; great is Your faithfulness. "The LORD is my portion," says my soul, "therefore I hope in Him!" The LORD is good to those who wait for Him, to the soul who seeks Him. It is good that one should hope and wait quietly for the salvation of the LORD. It is good for a man to bear the yoke in his youth."

[The above are a few of the verses that I greatly

value and I have often shared with others to help them understand the gospel and draw near to Christ. There are many others that are of great value and the entire Bible is God's Word spoken to us.] Luke 11:28: But He said, "More than that, blessed are those who hear the Word of God and keep it!"

2 Timothy 3:16, 17: "All Scripture is given by inspiration of God, and is profitable for doctrine, for reproof, for correction, for instruction in righteousness, that the man of God may be complete, thoroughly equipped for every good work."

II Peter 1:20 knowing this first, that no prophecy of Scripture is of any private interpretation, 21 for prophecy never came by the will of man, but holy men of God spoke as they were moved by the Holy Spirit.

Psalm 119:11 "Your word have I hidden in my heart, that I might not sin against you." Psalm 119:105: "Your word is a lamp to my feet and a light to my path."

I pray you will read the Bible daily and much and hide its truths in your heart.

Numbers 6:24–26: "The LORD bless you and keep you; The LORD make His face shine upon you, and be gracious to you; The LORD lift up His countenance upon you, and give you peace."

Much love from your Papaw,

Roger Bynum

Notes to Our Grandchildren

Our beloved grandsons and granddaughter, Aaron, Weston, Abigail, and Kellan: this is from your Papaw, Chris and Steve's Dad, Roger Keith Bynum. I love you very much and I wish I could have more time with you and had the opportunity just to enjoy being with you, but also to talk with you about some of the things that I believe are important about life and how and why we make the choices and live as we do. Your grandmother, my good, sweet, and beautiful Caraleen (Sue Baker Bynum), would have also loved to know and enjoy life with all of you. Aaron, since we were living in Mexico she only had three years to get together with you occasionally, times that she greatly enjoyed, and you were so young that I know you could not now remember. Weston, she loved you too, but you were less than one year old when our Lord called her on July 31, 2008 to come to Him. She would have loved so much to know Abigail and Kellan. I wonder if she sees us now; there is so much the Bible does not tell us about the immortal state that we will have hereafter.

This little book is about some values (ideas, principles) that are important to me and that were to your Mamaw that we tried to impart to your fathers. If I can help impart them to you, they will be the most valuable thing I can give you, but since Caraleen was such a special person and such a large part of God's goodness to me, I want also to tell you a little about her.

Caraleen Sue Baker Bynum, a beautiful, wise, and devout lady; wife, mother, follower of Christ.

The Bible says in I John 4:7-8, "—God is love.--" not just that He loves us but that He is love. I don't suppose that could be correctly said of any human-being, but Caraleen came as close to it as anyone I ever have known. I don't think she ever arbitrarily disliked anyone and chose to be his/her enemy. She demanded a lot of herself (she was a perfectionist) but she did not demand a lot of others to accept him or her and be his friend. She was kind. In the forty-one years of our marriage I do not remember ever hearing her raise her voice in anger. She was consistent in practicing the spiritual disciplines of the Christian life, like prayer, Bible study, church attendance, and giving to others. Caraleen was generous, always ready to help someone in need. She was intelligent; having the highest grade average in her graduating class at the Bible college where we met. She loved studying and learning. After Steve started to school Caraleen went back to the university and finished studies for a B.S. and later an M.

Ed. in elementary education and taught fourth grade for about eighteen years. She was never more satisfied than when she was engaged (with me) in sharing the gospel in word and deed with others, going many miles from her family with me in 1968, a year after our wedding, to begin a new church in NC, and thirty-two years later, in the year 2000, going with me to Guanajuato, Mexico for the same purpose. The most difficult part about it for her was being so far away from you (and your parents) and getting to see you only when we returned to Arkansas in June and December each year for the medical exams she had for 29 years as part of her on-going fight against cancer. Only one thing could persuade us to spend that time away from you. We were (and are) convinced there were people in Mexico who would die and be forever separated from God if we did not go and tell them the gospel of Christ.

Your "Mamaw" loved to cook for those whom she loved and she is well remembered by family and friends in the USA and in Silao, Guanajuato, Mexico for her delicious fruit salad, pecan pie, and other favorites that she loved to prepare. She also loved music and played the piano, accordion, and the guitar a bit even though she insisted she had to work hard   to do so and wasn't really good at any of them, but she encouraged your fathers and they excelled. Caraleen Baker Bynum was one in one hundred million and I will never in this life be able to understand why God chose to bless this unworthy man with her faithful love, companionship, and service. It could only be because He is good, He is love, and He gives good gifts to those who do not deserve them

Immediately below you will find the eulogy that I gave at Caraleen's funeral. Along with this document you should each have a small box of classic books that I hope you will read and absorb. They contain some of what I am convinced are the more important truths about living well in relationship to others, knowing, trusting, and serving God, and preparing for eternity because they are truths that are derived from the Word of God and thus from the unchanging character of God. I have also saved a bit of money for each of you that you will receive when your Dad thinks that you are mature enough to use it wisely. I want you each to also have one of my guns, one of my knives, and to be able to choose some books from my small library if you wish. Between Caraleen and me we had several Bibles (some bi-lingual) so you should each be able to have one of those if you wish. I have nothing I can leave you that is more valuable than the Word of God. It will do you good if you study it and make it a central part of your life.

Caraleen, my beloved wife

Roger Bynum,   August 4, 2008

Thank you, dear friends, for your friendship and support in the years Caraleen and I have spent in Mexico, for your help and encouragement in the times of her illness, and now for coming to help us give testimony to, and thanks for, the grace of God that He displayed so brilliantly in the life of my dear wife, Caraleen. One cannot really love Christ unless He is known, in an intimate and personal way; but one who knows Him like that cannot help but love Him. I believe to really love any person; one must really know him or her.

I think all of you knew Caraleen to some extent, but most of you only knew her in a certain context and for a few years, so you were only able to savour a small fragrance of the great grace that God poured out through her life. That grace was so exquisite that it should be more fully known. I want to try and help you know her a little better so you will love her and her Saviour more.

Truth is important, it is vital, and I am not given

to exaggeration, so I do not intend to compare any other of you, my sisters, to your disadvantage with Caraleen. I know your husbands who are godly and loving men would feel, think, and say about you things similar to what I say about Caraleen. But if in some detail she was lacking, in this moment I would have great difficulty in recalling it. When God made her He made a masterpiece. She was a beautiful, gracious, and erudite lady. She was my trophy wife. I was always so proud to have her at my side.

Caraleen was my sister in Christ; a follower of Jesus. Her commitment to Christ shaped everything that she was and did.

Caraleen was a disciplined scholar and loved to read and to study. I met her at a Bible school in Texas in 1966 where she had a perfect grade average until I undermined it by monopolizing her time. I was quickly captivated by her warm smile, her soft voice, her feminine beauty, and her quiet and kind spirit. She graduated as valedictorian of the associate degree program.

We married on June 24, 1967 and she accompanied me and worked with me in starting a new church in Wilson, NC, and later in a brief pastorate here in Sherwood, AR. When my theological struggles caused us to be ostracized from the denomination we had been with, she continued to love and honor me, and to study the Word of God with me to help me find our way through that refining experience. Then she worked with me in 11 years of house church ministry here in Sherwood, supported me in years of jail, rescue mission, and prison and counseling ministries, and finally labored 7 years with me in a church-planting ministry in Guanajuato, Mexico.

Following an earlier career as a secretary and bookkeeper, and her first diagnosis of Hodgkins lymphoma in 1979, and concurrent with her labor of love as a wife and mother, Caraleen returned to the university to excel while getting Bachelor and Masters Degrees in elementary education. She then taught for eighteen years at Harris Elementary School in North Little Rock for the Pulaski County School District. Shortly before she took a disability retirement in the year 2000 she received awards from the Arkansas Department of Education and also from the Lions Club for excellence and creativity in teaching, in part as a response to a grant that she and Mrs. Margaret Boyd wrote and implemented for a summer kid's math camp to inspire children to enjoy math and excel in it. Caraleen loved to learn and to help others learn.

Caraleen loved music. I can't tell you how many instruments she had, but she never felt that she was good at playing any of them, so she inspired and/or drove our sons to play and excel. Of course, when she drove them, she would drive one to orchestra in the Toyota while I drove the other to band or baseball in the Jimmy.

Caraleen loved to cook for her family and friends. I may be just a little biased but I will say "no one could touch her pecan pie, and her apple pie, banana bread, meat loaf, and cornbread were outstanding." When we went to the home of friends in Mexico and learned they had the flu, she would return home to make them cornbread and potato soup that she was convinced would cure most illnesses.

We came to Cornerstone Bible Fellowship in 1991 and soon began making short-term mission trips with others of you, first to Haiti and then to Chihuahua. Before long we became convinced that we belonged in Mexico working fulltime sharing God's truth and love, and when our brothers and sisters here at Cornerstone agreed and said "we want to help send you" we began our preparations to go. Finally in 2000 we were ready and went to Guanajuato but soon had to return for six months of chemotherapy after Caraleen developed tumors in her throat and lungs, her fourth occurrence of cancer. After four months of treatment she was so weak that the treatment had to be stopped.

In March 2001 she had regained sufficient strength that we were able to return to Mexico, not knowing how much time we would have to be there. Shortly after we arrived there, we came out of a hotel one morning to find three little ones sleeping on cardboard on the sidewalk under a fire escape and she said, "I don't know if we can stay here. I may give away everything we have." It wasn't long until she was talking about starting a campaign to rescue all the dogs that people put on top of their houses and leave there as watchdogs in the sun and sometime without shade or water. She couldn't stand to see God's creatures suffer as they all do from the impact of the fall of our first parents into sin. God gave us seven wonderful years in Guanajuato in which she taught English in our home and in the homes of our students and I taught them the Word of God. He gave us a ministry to area churches and in a nearby Bible school and I reserved time for individual, family, and marriage counseling appointments each Wednesday afternoon and evening at PIB Betel Church in Irapuato, Gto. He also gave us many precious friends who will mourn her home-going. We have seen many people come to faith in Christ, have baptized several people, and seen the start of a new church.

A few months ago while we were there in Silao, Guanajuato where we spent the last 7 years proclaiming Christ, she began having increasing shortness of breath. I wanted her to know how much I loved her so I told her that as much as we both enjoyed the Lord's work, I nonetheless did not intend for us to stay there until either of us were unable to travel and visit a few friends and places she enjoyed. Then just a few days before we left there in June and came here for her medical exams I recognized it was getting more and more difficult for her so I asked, "Honey, do you think it's time? Should we just wrap things up here and go over to Melaque (a little village on the Pacific coast where she loved to sit under the palms and listen to the waves at night) for a few weeks, and then go on up to the States and visit with our family and friends awhile?" She replied, "Well, let's don't get in a hurry. We don't want to quit until we finish the work God has given us to do." She never did quit, and she finished her work marvelously.

We returned here in June for her routine medical exams and learned she had colon cancer again and required a colon re-section. She spent five weeks in intensive care and was recovering from the surgery but was accumulating fluid around her lungs that the medical team could not control and finally her lungs failed. During the last few days many of her family and friends visited her in ICU and that was a great joy to her. Thank you, each one who called, came, prayed, or encouraged us, all in different ways.

Many of you will remember when she asked, "Will you pray with me?" Several of us spent hours reading the Word, singing hymns and choruses, and praying with Caraleen during the last couple of days, and she sang with us when she could. Once during that time she asked me, "Can we sing 'It Is Well with My Soul?'"

While in the ICU she had learned to suction the congestion from her throat when she could no longer cough it up but when she finally was unable to do that she would ask me, "Help, please." One time she said, "Hurry, please." Can you imagine a person strangling and being so gentle and unassuming as to say, "Help, *please*?" That was Caraleen; a gentle, loving, and godly woman. I know I am biased but I never had the opportunity to know anyone else well enough to know that he or she even came close to Caraleen's practice of Christian love and service.

Through the grace of God she ran her race faithfully and God called her home. What an incredible gift that God and Caraleen gave me 41 years of her life. Since she has gone there is an enormous vacancy in my life that will remain until I appear with the Saviour where she is, but the example of love and devotion she set was so lofty that I dare not slack in my devotion until I too have finished my race. Heaven has never before looked so attractive.

One Old Testament prophet said, "Let me die the death of the righteous, and let my last end be like his!"—Num. 23:10. I will say when the time the Lord has appointed for me comes, "Let me die the death of the righteous, and let my last end be like **hers**." God's grace in Caraleen showed us how to live and how to die.

May God be glorified in her life, in yours, and in mine both now and forever.

****

(A few days after the funeral I wrote this note.)

My dear wife, Caraleen Sue Baker Bynum, finished her terrestrial pilgrimage and went to be with the Saviour on July 31st, 2008. Before committing to the earth the perishable house in which she had lived, we met with the church on August 4th to celebrate the great grace the Lord had granted us through her life. On that occasion Richard and LaJuana Magee, good friends in our church, gave me a copy of the daily devotional "Streams in the Desert" by Mrs. Charles E. Cowman.

March 26th, 1967 was Easter Sunday and Caraleen's birthday, and when I escorted her to worship that day it was our first date. I gave her a copy of "Streams in the Desert" for her birthday. After 41 years the Lord used Richard and LaJuana to allow Caraleen to give that book back to me.

I met Caraleen for the first time in August, 1966, when we met with a group of college students in front of a church on a Sunday afternoon before going to the county jail to share the gospel. Caraleen, her sister Judith, and a friend named Marty were in the group, and such good friends that they were wearing identical dresses. I was assigned to the same cellblock with them and Caraleen or Judy played the accordion while we sang and I then preached. Years later Caraleen showed me where she marked in the margin of her Bible that I preached from II Corinthians 12:9, "My grace is sufficient for thee..." The meditation in "Streams in the Desert" is drawn from that verse on August 5th, the day after Caraleen's funeral, and at the end of the meditation are the lyrics of the hymn "He Giveth More Grace," a hymn she dearly loved and one we sang as we gave thanks to God for her life. I had never read the book before myself and only now am I doing so, and I had no idea of these "co-incidences" when we made plans for the service.

Our Creator orders our steps, all things are upheld by the Word of His power, in Him all things consist. I would have had no right to ask Him for any manifestations of His love other than what He has already given in the death of His Son (Romans 8:32), but He graciously granted me these tokens when I needed so desperately to remember that His eye is upon me, His hand upholds me, and Caraleen will be safe with Him until I see Him, and I see her again.

Roger Bynum

A Little About Your Papaw

When I began this essay I had not even thought about telling you anything about myself but then I remembered how I would have liked to know (or know more about) my own grandfathers, both of whom died long before my birth, so I decided that I should tell you a bit about myself.

My father was James David Bynum, a carpenter and a farmer, born in Caldwell, AR in January 1903. My mother was Mildred Ruth Thornberg Bynum, born in Ft.

Smith, AR in July 1918. Both Dad and Mom had been married before and each had two sons when they married. Mom's older sons lived with us and I knew them as my brothers. One of Dad's older sons died in a car wreck when I was very small; the other, Forrest, was a teacher and Baptist pastor whom I got to know as a good friend after I became an adult.

I was born in Oklahoma City on October 06, 1943 but my parents bought a farm near Wister, OK and we moved there when I was two years old. We farmed with a horse and a mule and our home was lit by kerosene lamps until electricity came to our rural community shortly before I started to school. I had the experiences of farm life and a small community and school until I was fourteen years old when my parents divorced after years of conflict and Mom moved with my seven siblings and me to Ft. Smith. My observation of my parents' experience caused me to be skeptical about love and marriage until I came to know and love my dear Caraleen. It also left me with a belief that a couple should never even consider separation an option, unless one's life is in serious danger, and never consider divorce except in the case of unrepentant persistence in adultery and/or abandonment. I believe these last two the only biblical grounds for divorce. The secrets to success in marriage are sacrificial love (putting the welfare and happiness of our spouse ahead of our own), humility, commitment to perform our vows, kindness, and patience.

I entered the Navy after high school and served a minority enlistment of less than three years just prior to the Vietnam War. After the Navy I returned to Ft. Smith where I began attending church to meet some girls but heard the gospel and came to faith in Christ and my life was radically changed. I quickly became immersed in the church and zealous about following Christ and preaching His gospel. Three years later I went to Texas to Bible school where I met Caraleen and after ten months we married. In October 1968 we moved to Wilson, NC to start a new church. There I received a Bachelor's degree in Sociology from Atlantic Christian College. In the fall of 1974 we moved to Sherwood, AR near Little Rock where I had accepted the pastorate of a church. That did not work out well so after one year we left the church and shortly afterward I began my own landscape business that I operated for eleven years.

During that time for over ten years we worshiped with a few families that met in our home. Your dad can tell you about those families who are still our friends to this day. During this interval our whole family was in school. Caraleen obtained her teaching degree, first a bachelors in elementary education and then a masters and began teaching. Our sons were in elementary and then high school, and I attended the university graduate school of social work in Little Rock, obtaining a Masters degree in clinical social work, and began working in mental health doing marriage, family, and individual counseling. Through the years when I served as a pastor, whether in a traditional church, small group, and much of the time in jail and prison ministries, I also worked in factories, doing construction, selling hardware and insurance, and driving a heavy truck, before working in landscape, and then mental health.

I had learned in my childhood on the farm to work, and later from the Word of God that any honest work to provide for one's family and help others is worthwhile. About 1993-94 I made two mission trips for our church to Haiti and then to Chihuahua to lead construction teams and also to teach what the Bible says about marriage, family, the Christian life, and church ministry. Those experiences led us to think about moving to Mexico to live, share the gospel, and share our life with the people there, which we did, beginning in the year 2000 with the support of our church and several other churches and friends. Caraleen served with me there for seven years before she finished her pilgrimage and, after a twenty-nine year intermittent battle with cancer, God called her to her eternal reward in His presence. I continued in Mexico for another four years, and although I loved the people and the work and still have many dear friends there, I didn't do very well there without my dear Caraleen. I returned to Arkansas in November 2012 to have more time with our sons and their families, and to try and finish a few tasks (like this one) that I wanted to do while I still have the health and presence of mind to do so. In 2018 I married Charlene Clay who had been a friend of ours many years. We are active members of Crystal Valley Baptist Church in North Little Rock and are enthused about serving God among our brethren there and also serving our Lord by serving our families and neighbors, and maintaining contact with friends and brethren in Mexico and in several states. We are very thankful for God's kindness we have enjoyed for many years.

Papaw, Roger Bynum

ABOUT THE AUTHOR

Roger Bynum was reared on a Leflore County, Oklahoma, farm and attended school and church services locally but did not come to trust in Christ until 1963 after he finished his service in the US Navy. He attended a Bible college, received a BA in sociology from Atlantic Christian College, an MSW from the University of Arkansas, and was awarded the Diplomate in Clinical Social Work. For some fifty years he worked on various secular jobs to permit his activities as an ordained bi-vocational pastor in North Carolina, Arkansas, and Mexico, spending some years working in mental health settings, and, prior to retirement, eleven-plus years doing evangelism, church-planting, and family counseling in Guanajuato, Mexico. He can be reached at lacmusa@yahoo.com.